MW01000631

Tips and Traps
When Buying
a Business

Tips and Traps When Buying a Business

Greg Balanko-Dickson

McGraw-Hill

New York   Chicago   San Francisco   Lisbon   London
Madrid   Mexico City   Milan   New Delhi   San Juan
Seoul   Singapore   Sydney   Toronto

1 2 3 4 5 6 7 8 9 0   DOC/DOC   0 9 8 7 6 5

ISBN 0-07-145797-6

This publication is designed to provide accurate and authoritative information in regard to the subject matter covered. It is sold with the understanding that neither the author nor the publisher is engaged in rendering legal, accounting, or other professional service. If legal advice or other expert assistance is required, the services of a competent professional person should be sought.

—From a Declaration of Principles jointly adopted by a Committee of
the American Bar Association and a Committee of Publishers

McGraw-Hill books are available at special quantity discounts to use as premiums and sales promotions, or for use in corporate training programs. For more information, please write to the Director of Special Sales, McGraw-Hill Professional, Two Penn Plaza, New York, NY 10121-2298. Or contact your local bookstore.

This book is printed on recycled, acid-free paper containing a minimum of 50% recycled, de-inked fiber.

Library of Congress Cataloging-in-Publication Data

Balanko-Dickson, Greg.
    Tips & traps when buying a business / Greg Balanko-Dickson.— 1st ed.
       p.   cm.
    ISBN 0-07-145797-6
    1. Business enterprises—Purchasing. 2. Sale of business enterprises. I. Title:
    Tips and traps when buying a business. II. Title.
HD1393.25.B35 2005
658.1'6—dc22

                                 2005017822

Dedicated to
Carol, Gregory and Doris

Contents

Introduction

Go Ahead and Make Your Day

If you have always dreamed of buying a business this is the right book for you. What is your dream business? If you could own any business, what would it be? Do you have doubts? Wondering if you have what it takes? Are you concerned about not knowing what you do not know? Worry no more.

Think of this book as your coach. You are the athlete and all any coach expects is that you make a commitment, trust the process, and put 100 percent of yourself into the game. Sure, it's a lot of hard work, but anything worthwhile is hard work. This book will coach you through the entire business-buying process.

Financing Is the Least of Your Worries

If you think that you simply can't afford to buy a business, think again. An established, successful business is highly sought after by financial institutions because businesses make a lot of money for the banks. Hence they will be eager to lend you money for the purchase of a successful business. New banks are opening all the time, so there will be many financing options available to you. If you have a 401(k) or an IRA you may also be able to use those funds to finance your purchase without exposing yourself to taxes on withdrawal.

Further, my personal experience is that most business owners are only too willing to finance the purchase for you. You can read more about owner financing and other funding details in Chapter 13.

Eight Reasons to Buy an Existing Business (Instead of Starting from Scratch)

1. Established Customer Base

With an existing business you get an established customer base. When you start a new business you have no customers and have to start from zero. So when you have an established customer base it gives you immediate cash flow. Which leads me to the second reason…

2. Immediate Cash Flow

You do not have to go through the trials and tribulations of trying to get enough customers to make a profit because established customers provide an established cash flow, a.k.a. money. With an established cash flow it is just a matter of managing the available cash to achieve your business goals. You do not have the extra pressure of finding enough business to pay the bills.

3. Experienced Employees

The third thing you get with an established business is experienced and dedicated employees. In the service-based economy of the twenty-first century, experienced employees are a huge advantage. They are trained, experienced, and have relationships with the customers. With a start-up business you are starting from scratch. Experienced employees can really make a big difference in helping you run the business, achieve your goals, and provide great customer service.

In the transition period, experienced employees provide a buffer allowing you to focus on familiarizing yourself with the operation. You will appreciate this time, as there will likely be things you want to change within the business. With these dedicated and experienced employees you will have time to make modifications while the business chugs along. This can be very different from a start-up situation, where you have to focus on getting new customers, creating systems and procedures, and getting the cash flowing.

4. Market Positioning

The company you are buying already has a market position and recognition in the community and the industry. Whereas, when you start a new business, you have no recognition or position in the marketplace. If nobody knows about the products and services you sell, they cannot buy them. Without positioning, you have to spend money on marketing and advertising. Plus, during the time it takes to establish your market position, you will be earning less revenue.

5. Proven Systems and Procedures

The operations, systems, and procedures of an existing business can make life a lot easier for you during the transition when you have many details to absorb. It is easier to make changes to systems that already exist than to create new systems from scratch or by trial and error. Plus you save time and money by not needing to train staff and implement new systems.

6. Better Financing Options

Financing an established business with established cash flow is appealing to both the bank and you as owner. It reduces the risk, and you will have better financing options available. On the other hand, if you are just buying the assets of a business, you will still need to demonstrate your ability to generate revenue, and you will have to pledge the purchased assets as collateral.

Another important consideration is that an existing business will likely have established credit terms with a bank. The banker would want to maintain a business relationship with a new owner. When you get to the point where you have a buying target and are ready to investigate banking options in more detail, have the seller arrange a personal introduction to his or her banker. Do not approach the bank without the permission of the current owner. Aside from being an act of rudeness, it is unlikely that the banker would disclose any specifics regarding banking history and credit terms without the seller's consent anyway.

7. Reduced Risk of Failure

An established business has a reduced risk of failure compared to a new business that has no customers, no cash flow, no market recognition, and no established trading relationships with suppliers.

Buying an existing business propels you forward (if successful) in a way that a brand-new business cannot. If a business has been successful, there is no reason to expect that it would not be successful once you take it over, especially if you can demonstrate in your business plan your vision and goals to increase the performance of the business (more on this in Chapter 1).

8. Seller Financing

One of the best reasons to buy an existing business is obtaining financing from the seller. Because the financing will be provided to the business (with your personal guarantee) it would not eat up your personal credit capacity. You will still have the normal amounts available for financing a new car, renovations, or other important expenditures.

The reason for business owners to finance the purchase is that it is in their best interest. They get the interest payments that a bank, investor, or financial institution would normally get if you went out and financed the business on your own. Just like the bank, they will have a note and a security agreement (i.e., lien) on the business for the amount financed. They will require that you also provide a personal guarantee that allows them to seize your personal assets should the business fail to meet its obligations. You will learn more about seller financing in Chapter 13.

Factoring in the Baby Boomer Demographic

The single largest demographic segment, baby boomers, are now beginning to look at retirement options. Depending on your view, this is either an opportunity or an obstacle. Baby boomer business owners' greatest problem is to figure out a way to retire and extract the equity that has built up in their businesses. For many baby boomers, that will mean selling their businesses and converting their equity into cash or retirement income.

Baby boomers have a liquidity problem that is created by one simple economic principle: supply and demand. Like anything else, supply and demand affects the sale price of a business. The more buyers (the greater the demand), the higher the asking price. Fewer buyers will result in lower sale prices. If baby boomer business owners all try to sell their businesses at the same time, there will be an oversupply of businesses for sale—meaning that asking prices will drop as finding a buyer becomes more difficult. The implications are vast. Without a succession plan or buyer waiting in the wings, baby boomers will struggle to get the full value out of their businesses. This will be bad for the baby boomers, but good for you as a potential buyer.

But baby boomers have another option. If they have not planned their business succession in advance, and they're unwilling or unable to liquidate at a lower price, they may continue to work well into retirement. With postretirement life spans of 25 years or more, baby boomers will need adequate retirement funds to maintain the quality of life they have become accustomed to.

If they have not saved enough money to fund that long retirement, baby boomers may decide to keep running their businesses into their retirement years. If this happens on a large scale, the supply of businesses for sale will drop dramatically, and prices will rise. This doesn't mean that potential business buyers have no hope, but it does mean that you will have to get creative to find a business owner willing to sell you the business that is funding his or her retirement dreams.

There's no way of knowing for sure what will happen as the baby boomers retire, but in any event their actions will impact the business landscape. For that reason, it's important to keep this demographic in mind as you consider buying a business.

Trust the Process, Make It Work for You

Buying a business is a big job. No matter what your background you can learn how to buy a business and be successful. The more experience you have in a specific business or industry, the smoother the process will go and the faster you will complete the purchase. Without direct experience it will be a greater challenge—it may take longer and require more effort. Is it possible? Absolutely. Be prepared to take your time, trust the process outlined here, and cultivate a healthy curiosity.

The business you buy will become the foundation of your financial future. Before buying, there are a couple hundred items that need to be checked and confirmed! It is easy to feel confused, and it can be overwhelming. In my experience, when buyers get overwhelmed they start looking for shortcuts. Do not fall into this trap.

It's All in the Details
Make a Strategic Plan

A strategic plan is simply a plan to plan. It is not redundant or a waste of time. A good strategic plan defines the game plan, rules of the game, and a process for playing the game. This book follows a specific process (i.e., a strategic plan) designed to simplify and demystify the process of buying a business. Take time to do it right and use this book as your guide. Take it slow and do not allow yourself to get locked into a less than desirable situation.

Do Not Skimp on Research and Planning

Business owners that I have met are all very good at what they do. They are highly skilled technicians. But when it comes to research, planning, and applying analytical criteria to making a decision, they either bypass it in its entirety or try it for a while until they become frustrated and skip ahead.

Read the whole book. You can jump ahead to find the information you need, just make sure you get back to reading the whole book so that you have a complete picture of the strategic and practical aspects involved in buying a business.

Do Not Agree to a Short Due Diligence Period

Do not allow yourself to be unduly pressured by the seller to agree to a short timeline for the due diligence period. Insist on the amount of time you feel you need. Due diligence requires about 30 days; 10 days is simply not enough time to get a good sense of the business situation. If a seller is that anxious and insists on a quick decision, you have to wonder what might be driving the urgency.

Practice Emotional Detachment

Unlike business brokers, acquisition consultants, and sales agents, this book has no vested interest in which business you buy or when you buy it. Neither should you. Divest yourself of becoming emotionally attached to any business until you get the keys.

Beware of Quick Decisions

In my experience, most people who want to own a business are generally conceptually oriented, strategic thinkers, and creative problem solvers. Once they feel they have enough information to make a decision, they move quickly.

Moving quickly to buy a business can hijack completing a thorough assessment of the business. That is why, even after you have made a deal, there is a period (called *due diligence*) where you can examine all the financial aspects of the business without hindrance. Without enough time you could end up paying too much, regret buying the business, or inherit unnecessary problems and liabilities.

Final Note

This book will provide you with the basic information you need to buy a business, covering all the stages from concept to completion. The accompanying graphic shows how momentum builds in the business-buying process and how this book breaks down the process by chapters.

For access to additional tools, information, and to get answers to your questions, visit www.sbishere.com/buyingabusiness.

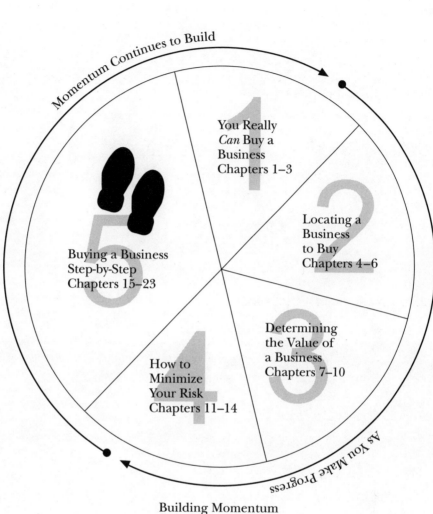

Momentum Continues to Build

You Really
Can Buy a
Business
Chapters 1–3

1

Locating a
Business
to Buy
Chapters 4–6

2

Determining
the Value of
a Business
Chapters 7–10

3

How to
Minimize
Your Risk
Chapters 11–14

4

Buying a Business
Step-by-Step
Chapters 15–23

5

As You Make Progress

Building Momentum
When Buying a Business

Tips and Traps When Buying a Business

PART 1

YOU REALLY CAN BUY A BUSINESS

1

Get Control of Your Future

If you want to have more control of your future, you like the idea of having more independence, and you have always wanted to own a business, self-employment may be just what you have been looking for.

Owning a business can at first glance seem to offer more independence. You do have the option and flexibility to make changes and do things the way you want. However, for every freedom you also have added responsibilities. Therein lies the paradox. The flexibility that you will enjoy as a business owner comes at a price. Your added responsibilities will range from managing your cash to making payroll, paying tax withholdings, keeping your accounts receivable (suppliers you owe money to) current, and hiring staff.

TRAP

Don't think that owning a business means unlimited freedom. When you're an employee you simply do your work, report to your manager, get your paycheck, and then go home. When you're self-employed, you have to answer to partners, shareholders, suppliers, staff, customers, and the tax department. Often the owner is the last person in the business to get paid!

If you are a really good entrepreneur and a good manager, you can end up with more money and more free time than most of the population. So if increased flexibility and added responsibilities is how you define "freedom," then owning a business might be just the ticket to living the life you want. Just make sure you are clear about your reasons for going into business and about the realities of the extra responsibilities that go along with self-employment.

The Key to Buying a Business: Preparation and Organization

In the process of buying a business, you will find yourself filling a variety of roles, including entrepreneur, manager, and, perhaps surprisingly, detective. Good detectives are investigators adept at obtaining information not easily available to the public. They have a nose for uncovering evidence, identifying information, and clearing up confusion. They exhibit a heightened sense of perception. They use tangible evidence, their five senses, and intuition to identify things that do not make sense. You will use your detective skills when investigating potential businesses to buy.

TIP

Do not treat the seller like a criminal; just utilize the tools of a detective to gain insight. Your job is to get the information you need to make a decision, and it is the job of the seller to provide you with that information.

Dangerous Liaisons—Believing Your Own Assumptions

Either you will be your best friend or your worst enemy when it comes time to make a decision about buying a business. The stronger your desire to make a deal happen, the higher your risk. Emotion can be a great motivator. It can also inhibit your ability to make an informed and knowledgeable decision.

As you progress through the process of buying a business, I guarantee you will make some assumptions about the business, your decisions, and many other related issues that may turn out to be inaccurate.

TIP

Independently verify all of your assumptions!

It is the assumptions you fail to check out that will later come back to haunt you. Ask yourself this question: Are you making assumptions based on what you want to happen and how you "think" things will work out, or based on specific knowledge or facts gathered from third parties?

When we make assumptions based upon our personal feelings, beliefs, and opinions, without verifying them independently, we set ourselves up for disappointment and failure.

Get independent, third-party verification of your assumptions with data and facts. One of three things will happen. Your assumptions will be proved correct, you will learn something you did not know, or you will be unable to find facts or data to support your position. Regardless of the outcome, the information (or lack of it) will allow you to view your situation in a new light.

Beware of Your Emotions

Emotion is a huge part of every major buying decision. Be careful to manage your emotions when making a decision to buy a business. Maintain a professional level of detachment; it will serve you well. Your role is one of a detective or devil's advocate. Beware when you start to justify your purchase decision and compromise on important issues.

TRAP

Excessive emotion from either the buyer or seller can kill a deal. The seller may become offended by seemingly innocent comments by you. As the buyer, remember you are on the outside looking in. The seller does not have to comply with your requests. Sellers should, of course, give you all the information you need. But if the situation gets emotional, they may become uncooperative or back out of a deal. Remember, they have worked hard to get where they are and are used to a high degree of autonomy. You will want to win their trust first, then ask the difficult questions and get access to proprietary information.

Planning Reduces Risk

Planning does not solve every problem. Planning simply allows you to make mistakes on paper rather than with money and time. Planning is only as good as the time and effort and energy you put into it. Think of planning as your insurance policy. The purpose of this insurance policy is to increase your chances of success at important points along the road.

Taking the time to adequately research, plan, and confirm those important points and assumptions you have made relating to purchasing your new business will give you bargaining power and set you up to succeed. Run several different financial scenarios, and analyze the impact these changes in your assumptions make on the financial outcomes. For example, increase your costs by 20 percent and keep revenues the same. Are you still profitable? Another scenario might be to reduce sales by 15 percent while increasing costs 5 percent or increasing sales by 20 percent while keeping costs the same. Taking the extra time to run through these scenarios will give you a "sensitivity analysis" of the business with regard to fluctuations in costs and revenues. Having the sensitivity analysis in hand is a big step in being prepared (we will discuss how to analyze business financials more in later chapters).

TRAP

The biggest mistake people make in business is not taking the time to commit their plans to paper. Are you one of those people who are always anxious to get started? It may seem easier to make adjustments along the way, but rushing a decision or being in a hurry can create a whole set of separate problems and issues.

Think about this scenario: Assume you decided to skip the sensitivity analysis. You buy a business and see that you need to purchase additional inventory to meet seasonal demand. You knew this increase in demand could happen, and based upon past sales history you assumed that you would have enough cash to buy the inventory you need. Except that now sales have been lower than expected. Your expenses stayed the same, and your total gross profit dropped along with sales. Then, as if that isn't enough, not long after taking over the business you loose two major accounts. Now your accounts receivable begins to reflect the drop in revenue, and you find yourself without adequate working capital to buy the inventory you need to meet the seasonal demand. But if you do not buy more inventory, your sales will drop even further. Now you'll have to scramble to come up with the money you need to keep your new business going.

TIP

Remember, the benefits of planning are deferred. However, some parts of a business plan will provide you with immediate gratification. A sensitivity analysis is good to have on hand should the scenario mentioned above happen to you.

Personal Sacrifice, Priorities, and Results

Being in business can be a rewarding or a hellish experience. Business buyers do not start out in business thinking they will fail. In fact, many start out with a much more serious fault: They think everything will go exactly the way they want. Often this type of thinking is a form of denial masked as confidence. But when pushed to explain their reasons and justification, they become defensive and fail to articulate a clear vision with passion and certainty. For all their good intentions, they just do not realize they may be on a self-destructive path of denial.

TIP

If you are suffering from the malady of denial (you may not be aware you are in denial), it does not mean that you cannot or should not be in business. It just means that you need a process and structure to maintain perspective. The good news is that this book will provide you with that structure and process.

One thing you will need to do to take full advantage of this book is to take off your rose-colored glasses and get ready for a dose of reality. Answer the following two questions:

1. Why do you want to be in business?
2. What are your expectations from the business (income, working hours, etc.)?

What are your answers? Do not skip this part. Take the time to think through your reasons for wanting to own a business. Answer the "why" question first. Then write down specific details about your expectations.

Arm yourself with courage, transparency, and a willingness to answer these questions as honestly as possible. Your willingness to be totally transparent and face the reality of your business situation separates winners from those who ran the same race but pulled out before the finish line.

Being prepared to face the brutal reality of your situation is an essential business discipline and anything less only sets you up for failure. It takes tremendous courage to look into the jaws of a potential business failure and see it for what it is: feedback on the actions you took. If you are unable to take corrective action because you are unwilling or unable to be completely open and honest with yourself, you cannot be open and honest with anyone else.

You cannot change and adjust to something you are not willing to acknowledge. You will end up sacrificing your integrity and eventually the business will fail to perform up to your expectations. If you are the type of person I think you are—brutally honest—not living up to your own expectations and goals could be the greatest failure of all. Take time to examine personal expectations and intentions.

TIP

Take time to write down how you feel about the impact the business could have on your personal free time. Make sure your family is aware of these limitations and supports your decision. Also think about your personal income needs. You should be prepared to take your paycheck after everyone else gets paid and quite possibly live at a lower income in the beginning than you have been used to.

TIP

Remember that you may also be risking your personal assets by signing an unlimited personal guarantee to get the bank financing you need to buy the business.

TIP

Be careful what assumptions you make about the time required for the completion of the sale. You may not be able to buy a business in the time frame you want or need. You will need to be flexible as closing on a business can be delayed for any number of reasons.

Six Phases of Business Planning

At the beginning of each year people start talking about New Year's resolutions. For the record, setting goals is not planning. It is goal setting. Setting a goal without a plan to achieve it is simply a fantasy.

So then what is a plan? Well that depends. Planning is the process of making or carrying out plans: specifically the establishment of goals, policies, and procedures for how you will operate your business. Increase your planning IQ by simply being aware of what stage of the planning process you are in. There is a difference between setting goals, planning, and writing a business plan. Here are the six phases of business planning.

1. *Research Concept or Intent Phase:* You are still trying to figure things out. You have a concept but there is still no formal plan. You are playing with the idea of creating a plan and are beginning to accept that you need to create a plan by setting goals.

2. *Design Stage:* You begin to conceive and construct an outline of the plan. Then as ideas begin to solidify, you put more form and structure into your plan.

3. *Commitment Phase:* There is a point when a commitment must be made to proceed or discard the plan.

4. *Resource Phase:* This is where many good plans go sour. You do not have the resources, time, or experience to execute your plan. Wait! Do not quit! Sometimes all a good plan needs is adequate resources and time to successfully complete it. Look for and ask others to help you. A wise businessman knows when help is needed and has the courage to ask for help from his advisers, friends, and family.

5. *Action Phase:* Once all resources are in place, it is time to take action! Take your plan and transfer it to your day planner or calendar, and create a timeline for each task.

6. *Accountability Phase:* A plan of action without accountability is doomed to fail. Find someone to monitor your progress and coach you through the action phase. Be prepared if things don't work out, but don't give up. Take a closer look at what happened, learn what you need to change, and revise your plan.

A good plan will help you improve and master any project. If you follow this outline, you will save time and be accountable for the outcomes of your actions. By identifying clear goals, tracking the progress, and evaluating your results, you will enjoy continual improvement and success. All you have to do is plan your work and work your plan!

Learn How to Write a Business Plan

Physically putting a plan together requires you to translate your thoughts about how you are going to run a business (and how it will perform) into a format that is dictated, in large part, by the industry you are in and the expectations of your audience. While most business plans share a similar structure and contain similar information, the content of your plan will be distinguished by characteristics that are unique to your operation.

Just as each person's resume differs because it reflects the particular life experiences of that individual, each plan will differ. But the format makes it instantly recognizable.

A business plan has a number of major sections. Each serves a purpose in the overall direction of your business and plan. The list below identifies and briefly describes each of the document categories that will make up your plan. They are presented in the order in which they typically appear. Don't feel constrained to follow this exact format if another way makes more sense because of the nature of your business. For example, the financial portion of a plan for an organization with a 20-year track record is much more important (and comprehensive) than the financial portion of a start-up's plan.

The mix of product and services to be offered can also affect the content of a plan. Issues relating to inventory, production, storage, etc., become less significant as the mix moves toward a purely service model. For example, an organization that relies on the services of professional employees would provide substantial details about attracting, acquiring, and retaining these key employees.

In any event, it pays to mention all the major issues listed below, even the ones that are less significant to your particular idea. Someone who is reading your plan will be more confident about your assessment of the situation if you identify such issues and resolve them, however brief a section might be. For example, if you plan to work alone and perform all services personally, you might note that you anticipate no need to hire employees or engage independent contractors if you succeed at the levels projected in the plan. However, if you plan to show growth beyond your personal capacity, then take the time to explain how you plan to cope with growth and recruiting the talent you will need. Remember; be careful not to raise any questions in the minds of your audience that are not resolved somewhere within the plan.

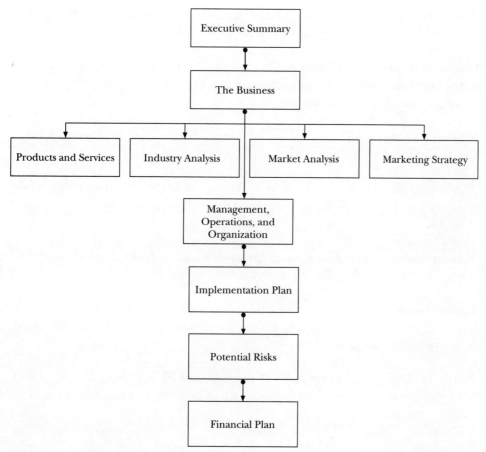

Figure 1-1 Business Plan Outline

Sections of a typical plan vary, and there is no requirement that these items need to be created or worked on in the order shown. In fact, you will likely find yourself having to switch focus to consider the impact that one part of the plan has on another. (Conventional wisdom has it that the executive summary, which is preceded only by the cover sheet and table of contents, should be prepared after the rest of the plan is complete.) A general outline for a plan is shown in Figure 1-1.

Executive Summary: Usually written last, summarizes and provides the reader with an overview.

The Business: Describes the company, trade name, vision, mission, ethics, goals, and legal structure.

Products and Services: Outputs, sales mix, costs and profits, expansion of services and product lines and product or service life cycle.

Industry Analysis: Trends, demand outlook, barriers to entry and growth, impact of innovation and technology, impact of economy, government, and financial health of the industry.

Market Analysis: Trends, size, competition analysis, projected market share, and decisions on products and services.

Marketing Strategy: Location, distribution channels, sales, pricing, tools: networking, circles of influence, Internet, brochures, sales systems, and database.

Management, Operations, and Organization: Organizational structure, responsibilities, and support (professional services).

Implementation Plan: Staff, staffing issues, systems, communication, bookkeeping, equipment, software, office, furniture, fixtures, land and buildings, research and development.

Potential Risks and Downfalls (Contingency Plan): Identify risks (liability, contract termination, etc.) and plan to reduce or eliminate identified risks or threats.

Financial: Start-up costs, cash-flow sensitivity analysis, cash flow and expenses, etc.

Selling Yourself—Hone Your Communication Skills

I have always been intrigued by the power and importance of communication. Now, more than ever, we need to hone our communication skills to build communication strength and endurance.

The race is on. Your customers need you to hone your communication skills. For example, your customers want to understand how your products or services can help them. If customers do not understand how your products or services will satisfy their needs, they will not buy!

Employees will need clear communication to accurately understand their performance expectations, so they can do their jobs effectively. Suppliers, from whom you buy products and services, need a business partner who can connect and communicate effectively with the marketplace. There is no other business skill that has more impact on your success. Every day, I see more and more that the quality of my communication directly improves the quality of my life, business, and customer experience.

TIP

Clear communication creates trust, which is the currency of every successful business relationship. It is during communication where value, trust, and rapport are created. Quality communication can create trust and powerfully motivate those receiving your message.

Communication forms the foundation of every business, social, and personal relationship. The real question is how many of our messages are effective and hit their intended target? By making modest improvements to the quality of your communication you can greatly improve your business results.

TRAP

Beware of the communication disconnect. A disconnect occurs somewhere between the delivery (speaker) and its reception (listener). Both the sender and receiver filter messages through their own life experience, personality, and beliefs, and each can cause the message to be misinterpreted.

Think about how changing the tone of your voice or your body language can substantially change the meaning of your message. Nonverbal communication is the language of relationships. Everything related to marketing and sales always comes back to believability. The way your message is delivered and received impacts your credibility.

Nonverbal communication (facial expression, posture, gestures) is the way we most often determine the emotional meaning of a message. We also communicate emotional meaning through tone of voice. Only a small amount of the emotional meaning is communicated with actual spoken words.

Depending on the frame of mind of a person you are communicating with on a particular day, they could attach a completely different meaning to what you say. Anything, including their beliefs, attitude, or stress level, can substantially alter the meaning they assign to your message.

TIP

Today, try to be a little more calculated in your communication. Observe the person you are communicating with and adjust your message to make it clear and easy to understand. See what happens. A little extra effort on your part to simplify your message could make a substantial difference in the quality of your communication and relationships.

Prepare Your Resume or CV

Now that you are buying a business, you may think that you no longer need a resume or a curriculum vitae. However, you will use your resume to win the support of others, particularly those who will provide your business with needed financing. Preparation of your resume as a business owner will be substantially different than as an employee. It should be modified to reflect relevant experience and skills that a business owner will need to run a business.

Think about this: People who will take a risk and invest in your company when others will not (venture capitalists) invest only in companies that have a high probability of success. See Figure 1-2 for an overview of how your resume might affect such investors.

Filing System

As time progresses, you will gain a lot of information that you will want to keep organized. Searching for a good business to purchase, you will acquire a lot of paper. A good filing system is crucial. As the process moves forward you will be amazed at how much paper will be accumulated.

Keeping it organized and accessible can be as simple as buying a portable filing system with accordion style pockets. I like this option because I always have somewhere to put the paper I acquire in my travels. Then when I get back to the office, I sort through it and practice the four *D*s: Do it, date it, dump it, or delegate it.

TIP

A three-ring binder with numbered tabs and an index page is also another great tool. It is easy to take to meetings, add notes to, etc. Plus, if you put the paper in the correct spot and then add the document to the index, you will not have to touch the piece of paper again.

	Probability Getting Financing	Equity Required
Experienced business owner Established business Established cash flow	100%	51%
Experienced business owner Start-up or business expansion	60%	51%
Has business experience Start-up business idea	20% – 50%	66%
No business experience Start-up with no cash flow	0% – 20%	66%

Figure 1-2   How Investors View and Rank Investment Opportunities

If you are looking at more than one business, dedicating an entire filing cabinet drawer to each business is a good way to keep everything organized.

The Electronic Method

I am old enough to remember using my first "electronic organizer." I loved it. I put everything in it. Then one day it died and all my data with it! That was before synchronizing software became standard practice to protect data.

If you plan to go the electronic route, make sure you have adequate security measures in place to protect the data. Of course, do regular backups of your data. You will sign confidentiality agreements, and you will never want to reveal the information you agreed to keep confidential.

Building Relationships

Buying a business is not very different from selling a product. You are building trust that may result in a close working relationship, at least until you take over the business. The golden rule—treating others as you would want them to treat you—is applicable. You need the current owner of the business on your side. In fact, when it comes to crunch time, you want the owner to really want you to buy the business. This could be very important when it comes time for the seller to sit down with his or her attorney. The seller's attorney likely sees his or her role as the deal breaker. Attorneys earn their fees by protecting their client, the person who holds the keys to your soon-to-be business. If the owner really wants to make a deal, he will simply tell his attorney to just do it. This could make the difference between your deal dying on the table or flowing to completion.

2

No Guts, No Glory
Things to Consider
Before Buying a Business

What Is Your Dream?

Since you are reading this book I am sure that you are one of those rare individuals driven to be self-employed. Despite this conviction you have doubts. If you actually bought a business, do you have what it takes to operate it successfully?

Well, wonder no more. This chapter will give you a fresh perspective on what owning a business requires.

Owning a business can be a wonderful experience. It will test your resolve, confidence, and force you to grow and change. You will need a willingness to accept a reasonable level of risk and a strong conviction and passion to endure trials and challenges that are sure to appear.

TRAP

If you think talking about the possibility of trials, challenges, and failure is negative, it is. Looking at things from all angles and possibilities is realistic and an important business discipline.

Face the Brutal Reality

The discipline of looking for potential failure is just one aspect of planning. Goal setting, research, and assigning priorities are also examples of planning. So is a positive attitude.

TRAP

A positive attitude is very important, but beware of a positive attitude that assumes success without looking at the whole picture. Positive thinking does not mean ignoring traps and the possibility of failure.

Excessive positive thinking, as I call it, can create blinders that prevent you from seeing the truth of your situation. When that happens you lose perspective and the opportunity to identify traps that could ultimately prevent failure. Always temper your positive attitude with a willingness to look at the "brutal reality" of your current situation, no matter how painful. Avoid self-deception and procrastination.

Maintain Perspective

Every business at one time or another will ride the fine line between success and failure. One of the most important skills that determines the difference is completely intangible: maintaining perspective.

Perspective frames how you view the events, circumstances, and situation you find the business coping with. It balances your vision, a view of your current situation, and a corrective plan of action. If you really believe that what you are doing is the right thing to do, just keep doing it regardless of what people say. Just make sure you have not excluded looking at the brutal reality of your situation.

TIP

Maintaining your perspective is the ability to maintain a balance between your current situation, your vision, and the appropriate action that needs to be taken. It seems simple enough, but there is more to it than meets the eye.

Here's an example of keeping your perspective. As discussed earlier, paying yourself last when money is tight is one of the brutal realities of self-employment. But let's look at it from a different perspective. As a director of the company you have a fiduciary responsibility to act in the corporation's best interest. Therefore, by making the decision to pay yourself after you pay your employees and suppliers, you are managing the assets in trust for your corporation and fulfilling your fiduciary responsibilities.

There are two types of crises that business owners often find themselves involved in. The first occurs when growth in sales volume outstrips the ability of the business to control its accounts payable. The second occurs when revenue is lower than usual and the business lacks the financial resources it needs and the flexibility to make adjustments. Both, surprisingly, deal with similar issues (staff, productivity, managing cash flow, etc.). The difference between success and failure is a matter of discipline and maintaining perspective.

Prepare for Failure

Part of maintaining your perspective is defining what success and failure look like. By preparing for both, you have taken the first step toward achieving your goals. Every business owner I have met is mentally prepared for success, but not every owner has a contingency plan in case things do not work out as anticipated.

TIP

Create a contingency plan by first becoming a student of business, industry, and human behavior. You can learn a lot from others in the same business. Sales representatives that sell the same goods and services to your competition can be an excellent source of intelligence to determine what is working and what is not. The actions you take in your own business are also good indicators of what is working and what isn't. The business will teach you what you need to know if you listen, observe, and take action. No doubt, previous management experience is priceless. But if you do not have experience, you will need to rely on your powers of observation and a tight management philosophy.

Evaluate the Business Potential

It was the stuff of dreams. History was being made as Spaceship One became the first commercial, reusable space ship to successfully go into space and return twice within a two-week period. The team was awarded a $10 million prize for their achievement. Now Sir Richard Branson has commissioned them to design a fleet of Space Tourism vehicles for Virgin Atlantic. Space Tourism—what a fascinating subject!

The very real possibility of space tourism will not only make Sir Richard Branson even richer but also more famous. Even if you have no desire to conquer space or become famous, the business principles are the same.

Identify an opportunity with little or no competition that people want, and you will have a profitable business.

Opportunity + Little or No Competition + Demand = A Profitable Business

Thoroughly Review the Business You Want to Buy

Buying a business is similar to buying a used car. Before you start to negotiate a price you ask the owner a series of questions, and then take the car for a test drive. If you are still interested in buying the car, you seek permission to take the car to a mechanic for an inspection and you review maintenance records to get a better idea of what you are getting yourself into.

A similar evaluation process for buying a business is referred to as exercising due diligence. You might hear the term used by your attorney or accountant. Know that the due diligence process will you give a better idea of the reasons the business is for sale, potential risks, and other liabilities. Due diligence is covered in more detail in Chapter 20.

Identifying potential risks and liabilities is a lot of work but well worth the effort. The more you are willing to dig and probe, the better you will understand the current state of affairs, which will then help you in making a decision. This book is designed to give you the background, questions, and insight to help you steer clear of the emotional factors in making a decision to purchase a business.

TRAP

Beware of becoming emotionally involved when buying a business. Your emotions could override your logic and hijack any serious inquiry or meaningful analysis. Emotions will also blur your perspective.

Maintaining a fresh perspective throughout the process will be your best ally and a secret weapon to defend yourself from being unduly influenced. Take your time, remain detached, and question everything.

Aside from the very important steps of exercising due diligence and valuing the business (Chapter 8), there are other ways to get a feel for how the business operates and what opportunities you'll be able to take advantage of as the new owner. Good managers also invest time to review customer purchase patterns. They use this information to monitor changes in customer patterns. One strategy I use in business-to-business operations is to review at least 300 invoices or purchases from the past two years. Often we can get a lot of this information from the business's accounting software, but if necessary, I compile it by reviewing internal copies of invoices.

With the information gathered from over 600 invoices covering two years, I create a spreadsheet with the following columns:

- Date of purchase
- Size of purchase(s)
- Frequency of purchases: total annual volume, etc.
- Returning customers vs. one-time-only purchasers
- Comments

When the spreadsheet is complete with all the data, I then sit down and review each transaction with the owner. As we review each one, we make notes in the comments field about the customer and transaction. For example, some questions I would ask are:

What can you tell me about this customer? What is unique about this customer?

Do you do anything special for this customer that you do not do for anyone else?

How did you find or get this customer?

Why do they do business with you?

We continue until we have reviewed all 600 transactions. I then review the spreadsheet to look for patterns, trends, and opportunities. This strategy has never failed to produce insight, innovation, and new marketing opportunities.

When you take the time to "probe under the hood" of a business you can always uncover new ideas, opportunities, and strategies. I have never met a business owner that did not know their business inside and out. The problem is that they never set aside the time to work "on" their business. They get tied up working "in" the business and do not make time to sit down and do a thorough analysis.

Before you buy a business, think about what new opportunities exist and how you can leverage relationships with existing customers (they are only too happy to get special treatment while you increase your revenues and profits).

TIP

Taking time to work on your business plan helps you gain more insight, reveals new opportunities, and increases your profitability.

Once again, planning is a profitable use of your time. It allows you to review what's working in a business, uncover new opportunities, and create a new and exciting plan based upon past success. I wrote this book from that perspective—to be a tool to help you uncover the information you need before you buy a business and use it to create your own plan!

Investigate the Industry

If an industry has seen a lot of changes, consolidation, or restructuring, beware, it may not be a good time to buy a business in that particular industry. If the business is in a market that is saturated or in decline, this could be a significant barrier to growth and unless you have a lot of experience in the industry, the risk could be greater than the reward.

On the other hand, if the market is consolidating due to growth, this could be a great time to buy a business. A market in the early stages of growth can represent a significant opportunity to garner new market share. Then once you have those customers, keep them happy. This makes it harder for competitors to enter the market in the mid-to-late stages of growth as the number of new customers starts to be absorbed.

Success Factors
Vision Plus Plan Equals Success

The difference between a vision and a fantasy is a plan. Without a plan your idea has no foundation to base your vision of success upon. You may have experience, knowledge, and a sense that things will work out. You absolutely need a strong belief and faith in yourself. But simply having a strong belief does not a plan make, nor does it guarantee success.

Taking the time to write a full business plan significantly increases the odds in your favor. The process of writing a business plan will give you the facts and data to support your vision. In the end if your business plan does not confirm your business assumptions, then you can simply quit pursuing it or shift the focus. I once had a client whose business plan, based on his assumptions, would have required a market share of 150 percent to achieve his projections—not realistic or achievable. By widening his vision and including a market segment he had not previously considered, we were able to increase the number of potential customers by the thousands and drop his market share to 1.5 percent, much more achievable and realistic.

Without the discipline of writing a business plan my client would not have discovered his problem until he had spent 80 percent of his budget and failure would have been just a matter of time. A business plan will save you a lot of heartache and pain.

Define Your Vision   *Couch wii*

Use your five senses to define your vision for the business. Determine what you want your customers to see, feel, hear, smell, and taste. Unless you are in the food business, defining the "smell and taste" is a mental process. For example, in my business I want customers to smell the opportunity and taste success.

TIP

Just put down in words what the end result of your vision will be. Define the customer experience. Then write out a small set of major goals to reach the end result.

Having a clear vision for your business will help you when it comes time to share it with your customers, staff, and suppliers. Even though you have not yet attained your vision, you can visualize it, keep it in front of you, and passionately keep moving toward your goal.

Share your vision with people close to you; try it out with friends or family members who you can trust for an honest opinion. In one or two sentences state your vision and then ask for feedback. Was it clear and did they understand it? If you cannot state your vision clearly to those closest to you, you will not be able to explain it or "sell it" to others. Work on simplifying it and making it more relevant. Strive for clarity and believability.

The Business Owner's Lifestyle

Owning a business is a lifestyle choice. Every business has a certain rhythm. It is that rhythm that impacts on your lifestyle, free time, and financial resources. Take time to make sure that you and your family are prepared for the impact the business will have on the amount of time you will have available for them and the other changes that can be expected.

Basic Business Skills

Experience in marketing, management, and understanding financial statements are required skills to buy an existing business or start a new one. If you do not have experience in these areas, a franchise might be a better choice for you (more on this later).

Understanding Financial Statements

The end result of bookkeeping and accounting are the financial statements. They are an accurate indicator of past performance. Is the business you are thinking about buying exhibiting traits of a business in crisis? Being able to interpret financial statements will allow you to recognize the "clues" of a business with problems.

You can find accounting, management, and marketing courses at your local college. Your local Small Business Administration office may also offer short seminars that will help increase your knowledge and skills.

Marketing

Marketing is the process by which information about a product or service is communicated to those who have the need, real or otherwise. The goal is to get people to seriously consider the merits of the product or service being promoted. A good marketing program will generate inquiries from qualified prospects (people likely to buy). These inquiries are a good indicator of future business and reveal how well you are meeting the needs of your target market (people who buy).

Management

One leading reason for business failure is inexperienced management. Generally, these people also lack the knowledge and vision to operate the business successfully. Certainly, as the business ages, management experience grows. But knowledge and vision remain crucial. In business, vision is expressed as "what could be" or anticipating the needs of the marketplace and filling that need. This is where new market share is carved out and innovation resides. Being able to see changing needs and market conditions allow you to anticipate and adjust your approach.

Your Background

Buying a business within the context of your career and direct industry experience is the best bet. Any business you buy will require a fair amount of day-to-day management. Your direct experience will help you cope, make decisions, and manage the business.

TIP

Simply having a positive attitude is not enough. Managing a business without experience increases your risk of failure. If you are unable to select a business where you have direct experience, and are still determined to make a go of it, work in the new industry to gain experience and see if you like it. It will give you a better sense of what you are dealing with. There is nothing as valuable as getting an insider's perspective.

Personal Issues

Owning a business is more of a commitment to living a particular lifestyle than you might think. The line of separation between one's personal life and business can easily become blurred, because you spend so much time thinking about and working in the business. Some outsiders look at some business owners and refer to them as "workaholics." I call it commitment to a vision.

TRAP

Commitment to your vision can create an imbalance in your life and shift from passion and excitement to a consuming focus that swallows up anything else. This can lead to family problems, personality changes, and health issues that significantly and negatively impact the business operation.

There are numerous stress-related issues that appear in the life of a business owner. Here are few of the most common:

Unhealthy Ego

It takes a strong ego to own and run a business. A business owner with a strong ego that also runs over people to get what he or she wants is destructive. Should you ever find yourself thinking things like, "Why can't my staff be more like me?" "Why can't I find better people?" or "Things were easier when I did not have to babysit my staff," it is time to review your attitude and turn down your ego. Take a close look at the causes of your business problems, not the people.

Family Problems

When a business struggles to make ends meet, the first to feel stress is the family of the owner. Getting paid last, skipping paychecks, or taking a small fee create financial stress. Problems at home can be a significant distraction and additional stress for the business owner. Get into counseling and keep the family informed of the business status. It might even be an opportunity to get some help from those that care most about you.

Sudden Illness

Cold, flu, or short-term health issues are just nuisances. No, it takes much more to keep a committed business owner away from his or her business. I am referring to a significant illness that prevents an owner from getting to the office.

TIP

Be careful and tread lightly, but the businesses of owners with health problems can be great candidates to buy. Often a business with an owner suffering a prolonged illness is in crisis. The sooner you can begin operating the business the less you will have to deal with later.

Depression

Many entrepreneurs suffer from depression and are not even aware they are depressed. Often, it is employees and family members that first notice depression. It can reveal itself through extended irritability, an unusually high need for control, and a loss of outside interests or hobbies.

Financial Issues

A business needs money to run. Beware of wasting your time trying to buy a business if your personal credit is poor and your net worth is negative (you owe more than you own). Banks do not take risks. They loan money to people with assets and a good record of paying their bills.

You could get an investor involved, but you will be giving up a majority of the shares (and control of the business) to get them to invest. Your only other option would be finding a business owner who is willing to finance your purchase of the business. While not impossible, finding a deal that works for you will be harder if you have financial problems.

Personal Credit Problems

If you have poor credit, clean it up before you do anything else. It will be a challenge to get the financing you need, or you will have to pay a high interest rate.

Credit Cards and Debt

Do not use credit cards to finance your business. You will end up assuming all your business debt personally plus incurring a high rate of interest. If that is your only option to financing your business, either you have not done enough planning, are not creditworthy, or your idea may not be worth pursuing.

Net Worth

Your personal net worth is important. You will use it to show that you have some cash or assets in the business, or it can be used as collateral. Why? Because banks do not take risks; they do not mind lending money as long as they can get their money back if things do not work out as planned. How do they do that? They will require your signature on legal documents that state if the business cannot pay its bill, the bank can seize your personal assets to satisfy the debt. This is called an *unlimited personal guarantee*.

Types of Businesses
Start-Ups

Starting a business from scratch can be a fulfilling and exciting proposition. It can also be extremely risky. The learning curve can be steep and require a lot of experimentation. Your ability to learn and adapt quickly will have a direct impact on your odds of success or failure. Your ability to recruit and hire key personnel to operate and run the business is crucial. It all comes down to making sure that you are comfortable that the amount of risk justifies the potential rewards.

If you have a strong entrepreneurial bent that just will not be satisfied unless you see your ideas succeed or fail, starting your own business can be a rewarding experience.

Existing Businesses

An existing business will usually have all the bugs worked out and have a "profitable formula" that you can continue to execute. Plus the business comes fully stocked with staff, systems, and something to sell. It will also have established relationships with loyal customers who want what the business has for sale.

Buying an existing business is an excellent match if you enjoy managing others and have appropriate industry experience. It will give you the opportunity to experiment and test your ideas to improve the business within the safety of an established cash flow. If you want a business where the groundwork has already been established, and you are a good manager and feel there is room for innovation to meet customer needs, buying an established business could be the right choice.

Franchises

Buying a franchise is not the same as buying a business. The franchisor owns the rights to the business concept, and you get the right to use their business concept, systems, and brand. It is more like leasing than ownership.

Generally, a franchise will have proven systems (marketing, operations, and financing) that you can simply follow and have an above-average chance at operating as a profitable business. If you are more conservative and do not have a need to put your mark on the business, a franchise can be a profitable and rewarding experience.

Most franchise business models rely on your ability to recruit, hire, and train entry-level employees. This dependence on young, mobile, and entry-level workers can impact your personal life. For example, what happens if one of your staff does not show up for work when you were planning to go home? You may need to stay and fill in for them or at a minimum find someone else to take their shift.

Because you will be dealing with entry-level employees, retaining long-term staff will be a challenge. This will make finding a manager to help you run the business more difficult. Your franchise should be able to help you with this issue, if they cannot, you may want to reconsider this franchise.

TRAP

 I have heard some people refer to buying a franchise as "buying a job" for themselves. That might be one way to look at it; just make sure you know exactly what you are getting into and what type of support the franchise offers. Know what is covered and what isn't.

Every franchise agreement I have seen expects you to pay an ongoing franchise fee. It may be calculated based upon a percentage of your revenue, a fixed monthly sum, or some other arrangement or combination. From a practical standpoint you will want to know what type of ongoing support you can expect.

Which Type of Business Is Best for You?

Your unique attributes, skills, and preferences will be the factors in determining the type of business that is best for you.

Franchise

A franchise will generally have a much lower failure rate than start-up businesses. Depending on who is reporting the statistics the exact numbers vary, but generally 6 of 10 start-up businesses fail within 6 years, whereas 8 of 10 franchises survive.

Franchise operations have a proven business model and there is no need for experimentation or testing. Not only is experimentation and market testing expensive, it is also risky. Newer franchises may still be fine-tuning so caution should be exercised when investigating a newer franchise. When compared to starting a business from scratch, a franchise can provide a safe harbor in which to refine your business skills.

However, a franchise is not for everyone. If you have the following preferences or qualities, a franchise would be a good fit.

Prefer to Manage

As the owner of a franchise you will be provided with a formula for success. Your job is to manage the "formula" and the franchisors job is to "manage" your compliance to their operational rules and guidelines. Therefore, a franchise is best suited to someone who wants to manage and has an aversion to risk and uncertainty.

Proven Systems and Formula

The goal of every franchise is to provide a consistent customer experience regardless of the location. An established franchise should be able to provide training, systems, and ongoing support. These systems will have been refined over time as they were tested in the marketplace. Systems will include advertising, marketing, operations, and human resources. If you have a need to improve or reinvent the systems and procedures a franchise provides, you would be better off buying an existing business.

Established Brand

It takes many years and lots of money to establish a brand name. The advantage of a franchise is your market will be aware of the brand. Trying to replicate this awareness with a business that is not a franchise will require a large investment and time, whereas purchasing a franchise that is a known entity significantly reduces the time required to penetrate your market.

Turnkey Operation

Many franchises offer a complete solution for facility selection, floor plan, equipment, and construction. In the case of food franchises, many have their own commissary where you buy your food products. Because they are buying for many stores, they get additional discounts that allow them to make a small profit while passing the remainder of the savings on to you.

Training

The most successful franchises provide training. Smaller franchises may simply offer an extended seminar, whereas the more established franchisors provide in-depth training in an actual setting similar to your own.

Starting a Business from the Ground Up

Trying to get on its feet, a start-up business will need to do lots of experimentation and testing. This requires extra financial resources, and typically the owner will not take a salary in the early days to free up working capital for critical business operations. Therefore, a start-up business is best suited to individuals with direct business experience, high net worth, and personal financial resources. If the following qualities or ideas suit you, then you should consider a start-up.

Being an Entrepreneur

What is an entrepreneur? Someone who organizes a business venture and assumes the risk for it. Therein lies the biggest difference between a franchise and a start-up, assuming risk. A start-up does not have a franchisor to fall back on and must sort through business problems itself.

The Hunt

The other thing that differentiates an entrepreneur from a manager is what I call "the hunt." Start-up entrepreneurs enjoy the risk and danger of doing something that has never been done or something they have been told cannot be done. They are part adventurer, part hunter, and part inventor.

TRAP

Entrepreneurs take risks knowing full well that they could fail. It is the possibility of failure that both motivates them and drives them to ultimately succeed. If this does not fit your personality, do not start your own business. Buy an existing business or a franchise.

Have a Unique or New Idea

Do you have a unique or new idea? Or have you simply recycled it? Not that there is something wrong with that. Just make sure that you improve it enough that it becomes a new product in itself.

Inventors

Obviously if you are an inventor, you will likely need to start up a new company. But there are other options. You could buy an existing business that serves the same market to leap frog into the market. If you see yourself going public you could buy a "shell" company that is already listed in one of the smaller stock exchanges. Then use that company to attract investors to fund research, development, and marketing. If you will require hundreds of thousands or millions of dollars, this will be the most efficient and affordable method to obtain the capital you need.

TRAP

Be very careful of companies that advertise to inventors. They often promise to review your product to see if it could be patented and bring your new product to market. Many are simply scams that are designed to get you excited enough to part with your money and never deliver anything of value that you could not do yourself.

Starting a Service Business

If you want to start a service business, a strength and weakness is that you generally do not need a lot of capital to get started. Often you may be able to finance the start-up yourself and maintain the highest level of independence.

Not needing a lot of money to enter a business means there are likely a lot of other people doing the same thing. It also means that you can get started without a lot of planning. Because you are financing it yourself, you only have yourself to answer to. That makes it a double-edged sword. On the one hand, you can get started quickly. On the other hand, human nature being what it is, we tend to shorten the planning process and just start spending money.

TIP

You cannot spend your way out of most business problems. You have to learn your way out by studying what happened and revising your strategy. But, if you spent all your start-up capital only to find out your perceptions and assumptions were flawed, where will you get the money you need? Who will lend money to a start-up operation that has run out of money?

Often entrepreneurs are innovators who tend to see the world differently. They often see what does not yet exist. Therein also lies their main strength: filling a need in the market. It can be one of the most exciting adventures if you are well prepared and have a business plan. It can also be your worst nightmare. Proceed with caution, do your homework, and persevere.

TRAP

Be aware that owners of start-ups generally work longer hours. You are the chief cook, waiter, dishwasher, and payroll clerk. Being a well-rounded, multiskilled person is a strength in this situation, but it can also be a trap.

Buying an Existing Business

Finally, we get to the whole purpose of this book, buying an existing business.

TIP

In many ways, buying an existing business has many of the benefits of a franchise without many of the limitations. You will be buying a business that is a proven entity with existing customers, staff, and suppliers. The hard part, the start-up phase, has been done for you. Systems will be in place, staff trained, and all you have to do is pay the owner what that person wants. You have an instant business. Just be sure not to overlook the learning curve and make sure you allow enough time for the staff to adjust.

Be aware of the following pitfalls when thinking about buying an existing business:

Hobbies May Not Be the Way to Go

While having a strong personal interest in the business can drive you forward, it can also be trap. Often people buy a business that is a favorite hobby or interest. For example, an amateur photographer decides to buy a local photography studio. He seems to be living the dream, owning and operating a business that he loved as a hobby. As he continues to operate it he finds, however, that the business is a lot more work than he initially thought and that working evenings and weekends shooting weddings and portraits has infringed on his lifestyle.

TIP

Your personal desires may override good judgment. This is why you must proceed with extra caution in a situation like this. Suddenly, you find yourself responsible for the business, making marketing decisions, and having to sell yourself. If successful, it will be a joy. But if your efforts fail, all you may have done is spoil a hobby that you really enjoyed.

Beware of Your Ego

A business needs to be more than a way to enjoy your hobby. Pay close attention to your ego. If you find yourself justifying your decision, ignoring logic, or short-circuiting your plans, take a step back. Reevaluate your alternatives and intentions. Make sure you are you really prepared to assume all the duties and responsibilities.

Develop a specific set of criteria you will apply before making a decision to buy the business. Reviewing these criteria when it is time to make the buying decision will help you make sure that this is what you really want.

Make Sure You Listen to Your Own Voice

If you are easily influenced by others, consider what their agendas might be. For example, a seller or business broker wants to make a sale; after all that is their job. Make sure you are following your agenda and not theirs. For more about making a decision and buying a business see Part 5.

The Benefits of Buying an Existing Business

I briefly touched upon some of these benefits in the Introduction, but here again are some great reasons to buy an existing business.

More Independence Than a Franchise

Buying an existing business offers more opportunity to set your own course than a franchise. You do not have franchise rules to adhere to nor do you have to pay franchise fees. You have the flexibility to make changes to the operation, rebrand, and begin selling new products or services. With a franchise you cannot add new products or services.

Another major difference is that if you leave a franchise, you will likely be restricted from operating a similar business for a few years. You have none of these restrictions when buying an existing business unless your articles of incorporation specifically limit business operations.

Established in Market

One of the greatest challenges in business is to become established, recognized, and respected in a particular market. A well-run existing business offers exactly that. They have penetrated the market and maintained a reasonable level of loyalty. Whereas, in a start-up every new customer is hard won, and the business must constantly build recognition and brand awareness.

TIP

If your sales, marketing skills, and resources are strong, you might be able to start up a business and make it fly. But the question to ask is "What if I applied those same strengths to an established business? What might be possible?"

Leverage Untapped Potential

Buying an existing business is not as exciting as starting a new business, but uncovering untapped potential and then making it happen can be equally satisfying and rewarding, not only financially but emotionally as well.

Existing Staff

Some industries have difficulty recruiting key employees. This is another great reason to buy an existing business. People are your most valuable asset. You cannot do it without them, and especially these days great service is a huge part of every business. It is the staff who create that experience either directly or indirectly. The right people create a great customer experience.

In the next decade franchises will find it difficult to find employees willing to work for minimum wage. Plus, there will be far fewer people entering the workforce than those retiring. Franchises will need to tap into the retired and semiretired market to find the workers they need.

Existing Customer Base

The business you buy comes complete with happy and satisfied customers. Depending on the business, you may be able to expand your offerings to existing customers or leverage current market penetration and expand geographically.

Full Ownership

Unlike a franchise where you essentially operate the business with the blessing and approval of the franchisor, you actually own the business outright. No franchise restrictions or limitations on your future.

3
Uncovering the "Right Stuff"

Only you know if you have what it takes.

I take that back. No one actually knows if they have the right stuff to own and run a business. There are lots of skills required in business. With growth the business will demand more and more from you. You will feel confident to handle some of the tasks, while in other situations you will feel that you are in over your head.

You have two choices when overwhelmed. Give in and avoid dealing with the situation (not a good choice) or dive in and figure out what information needs to be acquired, what support needs to be found, and what action needs to be taken.

Whether you have the right stuff to buy and own a business is subjective. The following 30 questions will provide you with insight into your personality and potential. Following each question are commentary and observations that you can use to evaluate your own answers.

Finding the Right Stuff Questionnaire

1. Describe how you make decisions.
   a. I start with research and gathering data.
   b. I discuss the issue with a trusted adviser, friend, and staff member. I think out loud.
   c. I only need enough information to make a decision. I am more of a "big picture" decision maker.

The ability to make business decisions is a "muscle" that gets stronger the more it is used. It responds well to training and yet is often overlooked. There is no right or wrong way to make a decision.

What is important is that you understand your personal approach to making important decisions. As long as your approach supports your management style, people will understand and follow your decisions. You are on the right track.

Those who answered that they like to start by "researching and gathering data" will fall into the "analytical" group. These people are able to consume and organize large amounts of information. When these types of decision makers have a lack of information, this strength quickly transforms into a weakness because they will feel uncomfortable making a decision and will procrastinate until they feel better (i.e., have the information they need).

While you are researching and gathering data, make sure that you do not miss out on an important opportunity or that your problem continues to grow during the time you are being analytical.

If you answered "only need enough information to make a decision," you likely pride yourself on your ability to make quick decisions. You have a sense of what you want to accomplish, and once you have information that confirms your assumptions you make an immediate decision. Your advantage is that you can move quickly and adapt to situations. The downside to your decision-making style is that every once in a while you get caught making a really bad decision. When speaking with these decision makers do not waste their time trying to sell them on your idea if you have not confirmed that they are interested. Otherwise, they will feel a lack of respect and dismiss your idea entirely.

Those who answered that they seek the counsel of a "trusted adviser, friend, and staff member" are in a unique league. Some of the most economically successful (wealthy) people in the world have a group of paid advisers (accountant, attorney, etc.) that they consult with before making major business decisions. They do what I call "thinking out loud" with these advisers to get a fresh perspective.

2. How would you describe your life over the last two years?
   a. Chaotic.
   b. Many changes and major life events.
   c. Mostly stable; a typical couple of years for me.

Hey, life happens. Purchasing a business is one of those major life events that creates stress, tension, and worries. Your ability to absorb and deal with stress depends a lot on your capacity to deal with the stressors in your life.

The more stress and changes you have endured in the last two years, the less capacity you have to cope with another change, taking over a new business.

If your life has been chaotic over the past few years, proceed with caution. Perhaps your life is on the rebound despite the chaos, and when you compare the stress of buying a business against the past two years and it looks manageable, go for it. The reason for this is that work can provide much needed structure in your life. Just be sure to not overestimate your capacity by creating inappropriate expectations of yourself.

On the other hand, if your life "has been stable" and pretty typical for the last two years, get ready for a shake-up. You are in a good position for the task ahead providing you are ready to run a marathon. Buying a business is not a sprint, it is a more like running a marathon. It will test your resolve and put every skill you have to the test. You will need to become like a chameleon that adapts to the changing environment.

Use this time to prepare for the long haul. Nothing of significance in this world is accomplished without training, commitment, and endurance. Think of this due diligence process as your "training" for the upcoming "marathon" which begins the day you get the keys.

Before running in a marathon you must prepare by gradually increasing the length of your runs until you reach the marathon milestone. Then you keep up your training by continuing to run to build your strength and endurance. The same is true when buying a business: be diligent, make a "to do" list with due dates. Purchasing a business will teach you a lot about yourself, the business, and market conditions if you are observant. Do not short shrift the process; it has much to teach you if you are open minded.

3. What best describes your leadership style?
   a　People say I like control and have an authoritarian style.
   b.　I am a person who seeks agreement and consensus among those involved.
   c.　I do not think of myself as a leader.
   d.　I like to work with people; to help them adopt my ideas and train them if required.

Are you beginning to see yourself as a leader? Like it or not, as a business owner you are a leader. Everyone looks up to a business owner. Everything you do, the decisions you make, and the way you present yourself all comes back to your attitude.

Your attitude is made up of your beliefs, feelings, values, and disposition. Everyone has a personality and carries a certain attitude, which is the seat of your temperament. Your temperament gives you specific opinions on the way you view the world. It is your "operating system" and forms your personality. Understanding your temperament and personality will help you work with others, compensate for your limitations, and work with your strengths. Struggling to think of yourself as a leader and demeaning your leadership abilities is an attitude in and of itself.

Choosing to sidestep your role as a leader means you will be relegated to follow others. The type of personalities you are working with will determine your direction. This is an abdication of your leadership responsibilities and has no place in a business. Those who work for you will wonder who is in control and find it difficult to be productive. Lack of productivity would frustrate the most conscientious employee left to their own devices; they will eventually leave your employment. If you are seriously looking at owning a business, you must deal with this leadership attitude before you destroy the business you plan to buy.

The authoritarian leadership style is another attitude that can cause employees to leave a company. Working for this person can be just as difficult. Authoritarians just want you to "do what I tell you to do" and in extreme cases they do not want you to think about it. They say, "Just do it." You can find this leader often interrupting others to correct them or show them how things should be done. They hijack learning opportunities and the personal growth of their employees, and worst of all, they rob an employee of job satisfaction. A balanced, mature authoritarian can be a great person to work for because you do not have to guess what is expected of you. They are tough task masters but you will learn a lot from them. If you are an authoritarian, just remember that not everyone has your abilities, experience, and perspective. Working on your communications skills by taking a public speaking course, reading leadership books, or finding a mentor can do a lot to substantially increase the communication aspect of your leadership skills.

Often people abused by an authoritarian will migrate to someone who seeks their opinion. This leader seeks consensus. Employees often feel this is a big improvement over the authoritarian style because it builds their self-confidence. But this type of relationship can lead to a codependence, where each party becomes dependent on the other for his or her identity. This can lead to a toxic relationship where resentments build over a difference in style and personality. The consensus seeker often has a hidden agenda, to seek the approval of others, which can interfere with making those tough but necessary decisions.

You see them in the workplace—people pleasers that talk a lot whether you are interested or not. You can also hear them flip-flop and change their opinion in the middle of a conversation. They struggle to form and hold their own opinions and eventually this leader becomes a drain on the staff, like those who have abdicated their leadership role. Employees yearn for a boss who is confident, opinionated, and predictable.

A true leader answers, "I like to work with people. To help them adopt my ideas and train them if required." Employees of this leader feel empowered, confident, and respected. Everyone comes to a job wanting to do his or her best. This leader is confident yet unassuming and helps employees tap into their hidden reservoir of knowledge and capabilities. They feel rewarded and appreciated. These leaders disarm others by their friendly and personable style. A business guided by such a leader will flourish and grow whether he or she is there to oversee it 24 hours a day or not.

I like what former British Prime Minister Margaret Thatcher is reported to have said: "Telling people you are a leader does not make you a leader. Leaders go quietly about their work."

It takes a strong personality and courage to make the transition to true leader. The good news is that leadership can be learned if old attitudes and bad habits are broken. The rewards are worth the price. Take a good look in the mirror and make a list of attitudes and habits that you need to change. Then work at them one at a time, one day at a time. Eventually, you will find that you and others are thinking of you as a leader and enjoying the fruits of your hard work.

4. What is most important to you when dealing with business problems?
    a. Let sleeping dogs lie. I avoid direct confrontation.
    b. I make corrections quickly. I make sure things are fixed and working properly.
    c. Before doing anything I prefer to investigate exactly what happened. Then I will make necessary changes.
    d. Being honest and maintaining my integrity.

Problems are not to be avoided. They are to be dealt with in a businesslike and professional manner. Polonius's advice to his son Laertes in *Hamlet*, was "This above all: to thine own self be true, and it must follow, as the night the day, thou canst not then be false to any man." There is an extra benefit in following this advice: If you always tell the truth, you do not have to remember what you said to whom.

Not only does telling the truth to yourself and others allow you to maintain your integrity, it will keep you healthy and make you wealthy. Everyone who has dealings with you will never have to guess where you stand on issues because all they have to do is ask. That being said, honesty can have a hard edge, especially if you are the subject of the honesty. In this case a little diplomacy can go a long way to soothing ruffled feathers.

Dealing with an honest person, you will never have to endure the wishy-washy style of someone trying to avoid direct confrontation. Avoiding confrontation is a costly behavior that wastes a great deal of energy and time. Confront them and they will either deny that a problem even exists or worse, give you a sense that they know all about the problem and are working on it but are not. These same people can also be great procrastinators who never deal with problems directly. This becomes apparent when internal conflicts arise. As a manager this person is a cancer to the whole team and should be removed from a leadership role.

Another style that appears to be similar is the controller that prefers to "investigate" before making "changes." It may appear that they are procrastinating as they take more time to make a decision, but that is where the similarity ends. These leaders are generally balanced in their approach to management as they realize that anyone can have a bad day. They gather the information they need to make an independent decision. They often wait before taking corrective action. Giving the parties involved the opportunity to take corrective action, which builds credibility while resolving the situation at the same time. If they need to make changes, they will do it behind closed doors or at times when the individual can speak freely.

5. Which best describes your beliefs about hiring people?
    a. Hiring and firing is a necessary management function.
    b. It is an opportunity to invest in the business by training and helping others achieve their goals.
    c. I simply hire to fill the vacant position.
    d. I hire people that present themselves well.

Hiring and firing is definitely a management function. It is also much more than that. It is an opportunity to serve your customers. Since the person you will be hiring will impact your customers' experience, the importance of getting it right is self-apparent.

What would happen if you asked yourself the following question: "How would my customers view this candidate?" Simply asking that question can change your perspective. It allows you to get outside your own head and look at things more constructively from the customer's viewpoint.

TIP

Asking good questions will give you a fresh perspective, but that is just the beginning. How you choose to manage human resources represents one of the greatest opportunities to improve productivity, increase profits, and simplify operations.

Every business today is a service business. You might be manufacturing an exercise machine, repairing electronics, or taking wedding photographs, but the delivery component is a service.

In the 1920s we were an agrarian-based economy where most of our gross domestic product came from the agricultural sector. That began to shift in the 1930s on when industrial began to overshadow agricultural production in our gross domestic product. By the 1980s the service sector represented a huge majority of all business outputs. The big three auto makers began to make more money financing automobiles than they did manufacturing them. Financing, whatever it is for, is a service, albeit intangible. It makes the tangible car or house a reality.

Since service is an experience and cannot be inventoried, your staff is the single greatest factor in your operation. Service increases the value of your overall business proposition. When a staff member leaves or is fired, you have to replace that person. It is, however, a real opportunity to spruce up your business, improve moral, and improve the customer experience.

Many business owners find the process of hiring staff laborious and frustrating, and many feel uncomfortable interviewing prospective employees. Asking yourself a few questions can make the whole process much easier. For example, what skills and experience does the job require? Make your list, check it twice. What personality characteristics are you looking for? A small business with the wrong mix of personalities can create costly distractions. Do not settle by hiring the best candidate when no one fits your criteria. You are better off not hiring than hiring the wrong person.

Business owner, know thyself. If you are a typical entrepreneur, you likely enjoy control. In other words you like to control things and have the ability to get things done. Be cautious hiring an employee with a strong need for control too. A small business with two "controllers" is a power struggle waiting to happen. It will not be pleasant and could be a huge waste of time and energy. Because as the two of you struggle for control, you are wasting time that could have been spent making money. Plus your staff has to wait around for you to make up your minds. For example, a better option would be to find someone with more of a "detail" oriented viewpoint or someone with strong promotional and sales skills.

6. What answer best describes how you feel about being in business?
   a. I enjoy achieving my goals. A business will give me an opportunity to be rewarded for my ideas.
   b. Business is an evolutionary process. I enjoy witnessing that change and growth.
   c. I love people and enjoy building relationships. For me, it is all about people.

How you answer this question will reveal a bit about your personality strengths and weaknesses. We all have them, weaknesses and strengths. Being consciously aware of them is the first step to managing them. For example, any strength taken to the extreme can become a weakness.

Weaknesses come in all shapes and flavors. For our purpose I am concentrating on the most important traits. Any one trait can be a strength or weakness depending on your personality. If you answered "enjoy achieving my goals," you are a goal-oriented person, confident of your abilities, and have a strong success record. You make decisions quickly and prefer the "big picture" and are likely visual. Your personal appearance is very important and above average. You love to be the center of attention and have a unique ability to get things done. Once you commit to a goal you are extremely focused and keep working and adjusting until you achieve it. Your weakness is in the details. You will want to make sure that someone is looking after the details for you.

If you answered "business is an evolutionary process," you consider yourself analytical. You must be organized to be productive. For you being disorganized translates into confusion and when you are confused you are not very productive. You can also find yourself digging for "more information" when making major decisions. You see yourself as smart, savvy, and a good problem solver. Your greatest weakness is that you likely think you can solve anything with time and the right information. While that is true, excessive experimentation based upon your observations and analysis can be an expensive trap. Inexperienced managers with strong analytical skills get trapped in excessive experimentation that studies have shown is at the core of many business bankruptcies. Be cautious and beware of analysis paralysis.

If you answered "it is all about people," you are a friendly and likable person. You are a great promoter and salesperson. You can get along with just about anybody and in some ways are a party waiting to happen. People trust you and you have learned how to make that work for you. Details are your weakness. You dislike getting caught up in details, things like writing reports, reading, and staying organized. Bookkeeping would be something you would either want to outsource or have one of your staff handle.

It takes all three of these personalities to run a business. We need someone who is good with people and a natural promoter; we need all details looked after; and we need someone who is in control. You will want to hire staff members to offset your weaknesses and support your efforts.

7. The statement that best matches my beliefs and attitudes relating to achieving business goals is:
   a. Play to win. Not a win at any cost attitude, but to make sure I achieve my financial goals.

   b. Make sure that no matter what the business will be able to endure and maintain operations.

   c. Maintain a positive attitude in the face of adversity or overwhelming odds.

   d. Manage, grow, and build the skills and expertise of the staff.

The purpose of a business is not to make money but to serve the customer and meet their needs. Fail to give them what they want and nothing can save you. Manage your affairs well and you will have a tidy profit.

Winning at all costs also means you can lose it all too. Improve your odds, look for ways to stay in the game. For example, do not spend your entire marketing budget for a one-month campaign. Hedge your bets by always having plan B ready. Then no matter the result you endure to play another day.

Controlling your emotions in the face of adversity is a creative way to ignore the truth about your situation. Face the brutal truth. Create an action plan that will give you an about face. Make a list of the things that make you feel uncomfortable, things you have been procrastinating about. Make the list, set it aside, then call a trusted friend or adviser and review the list with them. Ask them for suggestions on getting started.

Building employee skills is like an insurance policy that just keeps paying. It protects the customer and your interests at the same time. Having your staff take a customer service course, sales training, and public speaking program will increase their confidence and ability to deal with customers. As the staff members grow, they make a valuable contribution, and the customers' needs are being met and the quality of the experience improves. This all adds up to happy, satisfied customers.

8. Which of these statements best describes your personality?
   a. I enjoy achieving goals. I do not like salespeople who waste my time by trying to build trust and rapport with me. When I want to buy, I buy. I do not like to be "sold." Tell me what you have that can help me and get on with it.
   b. People like me. I love people. I am a good at selling myself and my ideas and have a strong ability to influence others. I am flexible and pride myself on my ability to adapt and change to meet current circumstances.
   c. I am a caring, kind, and supportive individual. I would not think of myself as a leader and feel confused when I do not have a plan or list of tasks. I am a helper and prefer to follow a detailed plan created by someone else. I am really good at my job. I love facts and data.
   d. I am a detail person. I consider myself analytical and am a good planner. Even though I am detail oriented and can create a plan to follow, I get lost in the details.

The Controller.   Controllers get things done. They buy the best of every-thing and are often in the top 1 to 2 percent of all income earners. They are unique and will avoid anything that is "common." They are very focused on their goals and confident in their abilities. They are highly visual. When it comes to achieving a goal and choosing to maintain a relationship, the con-troller will choose the goal over the relationship every time. It does not mean relationships are not important, just that the goal is more important to them than trying to make someone feel good. They often do not have a lot of friends, and you can track them through a jungle by following the trail of broken relationships they leave in their wake.

They make quick decisions with much less information than most. Their image and appearance are very important to them. What drives them is the need to fulfill what they know they are capable of achieving. If for some rea-son they do not achieve their goals, they simply make the necessary changes and move on. They have zero tolerance for people who waste their time.

If you are trying to sell or influence them do not try to build rapport; only if they are interested in what you are selling will they spend time with you. Just get down to business and eliminate the fluff. Be careful, though, they still want details, but prefer the "big picture" and make decisions once they feel they have enough information. If you insist on making them deal with details, they may interpret your efforts as showing a lack of respect or worse, not listening to them.

The Promoter.   Promoters make great salespeople. They get along with most everyone. They often make up things to stress a point and easily adapt to changing circumstances. A promoter is a party waiting to happen. They have lots of friends and love to hear themselves talk. The promoter lacks self-confidence and even with this extra ballast they seek out challenging positions like sales in an attempt to overcome their weakness. Sales gives them the affir-mation their personality needs as it makes them feel accepted and important.

Promoters emulate controllers and can appear quite similar. The thing that separates the promoter from the controller is confidence, or lack of it. They know they lack confidence, and you will often hear them voice it: "Well, I am just not sure," or "I just do not have the confidence to make a decision." When selling to them or negotiating, try to align your proposal with someone you know they respect (another controller or successful person). They buy anything sexy, trendy, or whatever controllers buy. When they miss a goal, they view it as their fault and ruminate over it, driving their confidence lower.

The Supporter.   Supporters are quiet, unassuming, and the helpers of the world. Ask them to do something, and they will often set their own agenda aside to help you. They focus a lot of time and energy on building and maintaining relationships. In a group they are shy and quiet. Although they are not outspoken, they form strong opinions; it just takes a lot to get them to express it. Once they feel comfortable with you, they will carry on a conversation; just do not expect them to initiate it. If they know you they love you and can be loyal to a fault. A supporter will always preserve a relationship, even at the expense of not achieving their own goals. These people buy traditional cars, recycle, and are intelligent. Ideal occupations include customer service, inside sales, and management.

The Analyzer.   With strong analytical skills the analyzer loves data and is hard working. They are well organized and detail oriented. Analyzers drive controllers crazy. Both in length of time it takes them to make a decision and the amount of detail they need to make it. Their need for information is far more than a controller would need. Information is important because they like to make smart decisions. They do not want to be corrupted by "the system" and are ferociously independent. They pride themselves on their personal integrity and are socially conscious. They get involved in current affairs, environmental concerns, and the homeless. Their attention to detail supports the controller who is not detail oriented. Working in seclusion is not a problem for them whereas promoters would explode if they did not have someone to party or talk with. Occupations often include lawyers, accountants, engineers, and physicians.

You should base your selection and hiring of people in accordance with your own personality and style. Find people who are different. As counterintuitive as that might sound, it is a sound business strategy. It will add balance to the business and support achieving your goals.

9. When completing a long and difficult project I tend to:
    a. Get it finished ASAP.
    b. Procrastinate finishing a project.
    c. Review progress to date.
    d. Look for opportunities to overdeliver and exceed customer expectations.

I used to be a starter. I was working 14 to 18 hours a day on three different businesses and starting two others. It was insane but I relished it. I loved the variety of working on something different every few hours. Plus I got to see my ideas come to life. There was just one problem. I struggled to complete what I started. This was not a problem for me, but it became a problem for the customer.

In those days I was a craftsman. I knew my craft and was willing to take on almost any project especially if I had the opportunity to learn something new. It was both rewarding and scary. I learned so much about how not to run a business. The anxiety and stress I endured was not healthy. Coming close to a deadline I was anxious which made it difficult for everyone in my life. I got the work done but was hard on people. The quality was pretty good but not outstanding. Did the customers get what they paid for? Absolutely. Where they exceedingly happy and impressed? Was I getting referrals? No, referrals did not come despite the fact that I produced a good product. It has taken years for me to learn how to underpromise and overdeliver.

Now I strive to finish well. I am a student of my craft with an eye for detail, a master craftsman. What is the difference between a master boat builder and a journeyman boat builder? It all comes down to an eye for detail. Both studied the same material, received the same training, and know how to design and build boats. The difference is that the master craftsman is constantly honing his skills and is a student of his craft. The other major difference can be seen in the finished product. Side by side, you see the difference in the finishing details.

To the master craftsman the finished work becomes the ultimate expression of his passion. He is driven to produce a finished product that he is proud to affix his name to. He will redo, rework, and rebuild it until he gets it just the way he envisioned. He holds himself to his own standard of excellence. Referrals come easily as customers are so pleased with the final product. They often use terms like "He exceeded all my expectations," or "I am so proud of my boat. It is a work of art."

When I had so many projects and businesses on the go I had lots of good reasons to justify why some of the important details were left out. Yet I could not say that we were really successful. Even though I wondered: who was as busy as me? Who had that many projects on the go? What I discovered shocked me.

It was a way to avoid responsibility. The problem? I was not committed to any one project. I did not have to "make it or break it" because when the going got tough, I simply diverted my attention to a different project. Kind of like a breakfast of ham and eggs. The chicken is involved but the pig is really committed. Like the chicken I too had an escape. The backdoor was in the form of pet projects. They were there to keep me busy, skirt the truth, and avoid anything that looked like accountability. I became a "jack of all trades" and a master of none.

Fortunately, my knowledge (I have worked in over 30 different industries) has become a real asset. But I have also restricted my business activities to business planning, writing, and training.

Today, I get great referrals and plenty of compliments. Most important I have my own written definition and standard of excellence and craftsmanship that I hold myself accountable to. I am proud of my work and am able to call my customers friends.

What are your standards? How do you define success? What are the principles you believe in? What is your code of conduct, i.e., morals, ethics? How will you measure your performance? To whom are you accountable?

If you do not have a written code of conduct, you cannot hold yourself accountable to a higher standard. It is natural human behavior to find shortcuts or ways to work around a difficult task. Until you have a written code of conduct by which hold yourself accountable, you will always have a "back door" as an escape to avoid true accountability.

10. Delegation is something I do to:
    a. Get stuff off my list.
    b. Put the best person on the job.
    c. Extend my authority to a subordinate.
    d. Download responsibilities.

Delegating key tasks to subordinates empowers employees, increases job satisfaction, and is a great example of leadership. A business grows in direct proportion to the personal growth of its employees. If the members of your staff stagnate, become bored, and stop giving their best, your business will suffer.

Like any management tool, delegation can be abused. In absence of a clear purpose, delegating tasks that you do not want to do or do not have time to do is not an enlightened perspective. The purpose of delegation should have as its core motivation, management, and leadership.

If you start to think of your management philosophy as "organized delegation," then your perspective on management will shift from one of downloading of tasks to extending your authority and responsibilities to employees. It allows employees to make decisions based upon criteria and boundaries you define. Plus it also gives employees the opportunity to "be at the center" of the action while extending your reach without being directly involved in the situation.

TIP

One of the things employees want most from their job is autonomy. They want to see that they are making a direct contribution to the health and vitality of the business. This gives them a feeling that they are important, that their work matters, and that they are capable and trustworthy.

Autonomy without accountability and responsibility demotes its importance and is like having a bunch of robots running around doing what they are told. Not exactly the picture of a company that is passionate and excited about serving and meeting customer needs. Anyone can delegate and download tasks. Not everyone can lead, empower, and build passion in the hearts of employees. It requires leadership and the ability to see the bigger picture and purpose of the business. Because a big part of the reward is in the work itself and through enlightened delegation, you can train, empower, and reward employees while getting important tasks accomplished.

Most importantly it extends your authority to the employee and by example teaches important leadership lessons. There is no better outcome to delegation than to know that you have a leader in waiting. This type of employee gives you peace of mind, so you can enjoy vacations. Leader, begets leader, begets leader. Enlightened, empowered, and excited employees sounds like a profitable business venture to me!

11. In my opinion a business can best be described as (pick one answer only):
     a. Straight line.
     b. Circle.
     c. Military operation.
     d. Fluid.

When I ask people to define a business using a graphic symbol most come up with some sort of chart with a steady upward trend in revenue, using a straight line. Most businesses never attain this ideal of consistent, measured growth.

Business is fluid. Like water it seeks its own level and fills lower elevations with its presence. A series of puddles that eventually form a pond, then a lake, and finally a river that ends up at the source, an ocean of opportunities.

Like all nature the ocean has an ebb and flow. The receding and rising tidal waters are cyclical and natural. The same is true of a business. It follows a natural ebb and flow. It is much easier to go clam and crab picking when the tide is out, and it is the best time to harvest clams and crab because they are much easier to catch. The same is true of a business: there are times when you have to work much harder to get the same results because you often cannot wait for the tide to change. Answer this question: What is the natural flow of the business you are interested in purchasing?

It really does not matter what your answer is to this question; the point I want to make is that if you pay attention to the natural ebb and flow of the business, you will be able to shift and adjust your strategy.

If you are out of sync with the natural ebb and flow of a business, you will spend valuable resources when you have the least chance at success. It is like gambling with the odds significantly weighted against you.

TIP

You can put the odds in your favor by paying attention to natural changes and business cycles.

For example, resource-based economies follow a 10-year boom-and-bust cycle, while service based economies follow a 4-year boom-and-bust cycle. During a bust cycle you will need to change your strategy and tactics to meet the current economic and business realities.

Identify the signs of change in the business you are buying. Find out what the impact to the business will be. Create a strategy in advance to cope and adjust with the boom and bust realities. If you feel you are coming out of a bust, plan ahead to add resources, inventory and staff. If you think the boom has busted, it is time to reduce expenses. Take time to evaluate what you can do without or how you can eliminate expenses.

12. When starting something new, I:
    a. Get into action quickly and figure it out as I go. I like to experiment, try new ideas, and evolve.
    b. Like to familiarize myself with the people involved then work out the details.
    c. Start by gathering information before I begin working on a project.
    d. Think about it then decide how to best go about the task before wasting time on irrelevant tasks. I plan my work and work my plan.

Experimentation is a part of business, but if excessive, can increase your risk to where you put the business in jeopardy. Studies of business failures list excessive experimentation as one of the main reasons new businesses go bankrupt.

Depending on your personality your answer to this question reflects your natural tendencies. For example, if you are analytical you likely answered *c* and the controllers reading this book likely answered *d*. Since the promoter just wants to get going and loves flexibility, they will have answered *a*. For supporters, their need for connection with others finds them answering *b*.

Everyone has an analytical, promoter, supporter, and controller side to their personality. If you have answered all of the above questions, then you are a true analytical, the one trying to figure out why I am asking you all these questions and how answering these questions is going to help you. The answer is the better you know your strengths and weaknesses the more you can adapt and grow.

13. I consider myself a person who likes:
    a. Flexibility.
    b. Working with others.
    c. Control and structure.
    d. Considering all my options.

No one likes to be controlled. Yet control is important for human beings. Some use different means to gain and maintain control. Where the analyzer controls through the use of information, the supporter gets control being in a relationship and by getting to know people. Promoters control their environment by finessing and controlling people by influencing others and getting them to do what they need them to do.

Controllers do not hide that they are in control and that they have certain expectations of others. For some, the controller is a formidable adversary to be avoided. The controller's confidence causes promoters to doubt themselves and their abilities. The supporter just wants to get along and have a relationship, while the controller has not given the relationship a second thought.

There is no right or wrong. You are who you are, and depending on what is going on in your life, you will transition in and out of each personality type when you need to. However, we all have a natural tendency to gravitate toward one type. Controllers will feel they can be a promoters, analyzers, and supporters. But they are better at being a controller than anyone else.

14. When I observe something being done incorrectly, I:
    a. Let the person figure it out.
    b. Discipline the person involved.
    c. Wait for an opportunity to help the person see the error.
    d. Stop the person and show him or her how to do it correctly.

Job hijacking happens more than you think. When the boss stops an employee in the process of doing a task, takes it over or sends them to do something else, you have just witnessed a job hijack in progress. It is frustrating for the poor employee because they have been robbed of the opportunity to learn something and the satisfaction of figuring something out and doing their job.

Discipline is not always the best approach to making sure things get done correctly. Because eventually an employee who is constantly being corrected gets tired of getting corrected all the time. Without a change they will likely quit and move on to another job.

The most productive and enlightened strategy is to wait for the right time to help the person involved to see the error of their ways; then they will naturally take corrective action.

Simply letting someone figure it out is a passive approach to management, and unless the person has their own high standards and a strong work ethic, you cannot expect much. People naturally rise to a challenge and managing passively is not a challenge for you or the employee. Raise the bar!

15. I lead by:
    a. Explaining my expectations, then leave them to figure out how to do it.
    b. Helping others set meaningful goals.
    c. Example and expect them to emulate accordingly.
    d. Creating and managing a project then assigning roles and responsibilities.

There are many of different ways to lead. The first step is to acknowledge that you are a leader. Setting the vision for the company is your first priority. Vision is what you will become or where you will go, whereas a mission statement is how you plan to fulfill the vision. The vision should be specific, exciting, and attainable. Do not make people guess or have to interpret your vision. If you cannot make it clear, exciting, and understandable, you need to keep working on it.

By helping others set meaningful goals, you look after everything. The right people, pursuing the right goals, will get a lot done, and they will not need a lot of supervision. They just get the work done. Now that's leadership!

16. People who know me well would say that, when confronted with a tough decision, I:
    a. Seek out input and opinions from others.
    b. Change my mind and priorities a lot.
    c. Base my decisions upon what I think and believe. All that matters is what I think.
    d. Procrastinate making a decision or commitment.

Another important aspect of leadership is your decision-making ability. You cannot delegate decisions about direction, vision, and strategy. As owner you have the ultimate responsibility to act in the company's best interest. There will be times when a tough decision needs to be made. Getting opinions and input from others may provide you with moral support, but the decision is yours to live with.

If you procrastinate, set deadlines for yourself. Define what criteria you will use to make your decision before attempting changes. Some decisions are simple. Anything that will threaten the viability of the business must be dealt with quickly, and your decision must always be in the best interest of the business. This may be in direct contrast to what your personal priorities would dictate. Regardless, you need to make the decision that is in the best interest of the business even if it costs you personally or financially. Forgoing a paycheck to make payroll or paying the bills hurts in the short term but is a good business decision. This not only preserves your integrity but protects you against lawsuits from shareholders, IRS actions, and bankers or investors. Plus people know they can count on you to do the right thing and that builds your reputation.

I hope you did not answer "All that matters is what I think." Because in business nothing could be further from the truth. You cannot work in a vacuum and succeed in business.

If you tend to change your mind a lot, that indicates a lack of confidence; if you are a promoter, that is a natural state for you. However, indecision can damage the business and frustrate your staff. You often have to make decisions without enough information or as much time as you would like. Making decisions is a skill that can be acquired.

Depending on your personality seeking the "opinions of others" can be a way to avoid making a decision. It is also something that can be used to avoid accountability.

17. When it comes to reading financial statements:
     a. As long as I know my bank balance I am happy. What is a financial statement?
     b. I have a basic understanding of financial statements but would not be able to confidently interpret the results.
     c. I am familiar with financial statements and can interpret the meaning.

Financial statements are a reflection of what happened in the business in the past. They reflect every decision you made and reveal how every dollar was spent. Being able to interpret financial statements is a very important business skill. Many colleges offer evening accounting courses.

As your business grows your financial statements become increasingly important. Banks will use them to determine the financial health of the business and your ability to repay a loan.

When you buy a business, you will need to hire an accountant to review financial statements for liabilities and due diligence. For example, if you are doing a stock purchase, having your CPA examine financial statements is especially important to determine any outstanding or potential liabilities. Because when you do a stock purchase you assume all the liabilities of the company. This would include any discrepancies in tax returns or creative bookkeeping that could arise out of an IRS audit. Examine potential environmental issues that may become critical in the future.

18. In my opinion business plans are:
    a. Helpful.
    b. Absolutely required. I would be lost without one.
    c. I would likely only write a business plan if the bank asks me for one.
    d. Business plans are a lot of work and not as useful as actually working on the business.

My first business plan was like giving blood. I knew I should give blood, but getting to the point of actually doing it gave rise to the procrastinator in me. I am not different than other people: I avoid doing the things I do not like. Writing a business plan was one of those things I knew I needed, but it seemed like a lot of work and what use would it be to me?

I had no idea how valuable the process of committing my plans to writing would become. I tried all sorts of shortcuts using templates and software that was supposed to simplify the process; but I still found that something was lacking, and I did not feel confident with the content of my business plan.

I discovered that the shortcomings I experienced writing a business plan were not that much different than what most people experienced. In the beginning I did not understand financial statements, and when I looked at samples of pro forma financial projections I felt overwhelmed. Add to that the lack of structure and a guide to help me navigate the sea of words, I was intimidated. The other stumbling block was that I did not know what I know. There was important information stuck in my head that I did not know needed to be in the business plan. Put it all together and the whole thing seemed daunting. I found myself in procrastination mode, which came with a fair bit of guilt because I had made a promise to myself that I would "do it right" and complete a business plan.

So to fill the gap I wrote *The Business Plan Coach* to be my coach and guide. I discovered that no matter how complicated the business plan became *The Business Plan Coach* kept me on track. *The Business Plan Coach* is available to guide you through the business plan maze. You can find more information at my Web site, www.sbishere.com. Benefits include:

- Tapping into concealed knowledge you already possess for use in your business plan.

- Gaining an understanding of the importance of each section of a business plan.

- Utilizing the business plan in the real world of day-to-day business.

- Eliminating roadblocks and navigating intricacies of a business plan.

19. Being in business is important because:
    a. I want to be more independent.
    b. I like meeting the needs of a marketplace.
    c. I am buying myself a job.
    d. I need something to do to make money in semiretirement or retirement.

Stop referring to yourself as the owner or manager. Become the steward—an individual who is in charge of managing the affairs of someone else. As a company director the law states you are obligated to put the company's needs ahead of your own.

I was sitting in John's office beginning a consulting engagement when he revealed that he had spent two years in jail. He was the director of a company whose manager had embezzled $100,000 and left the country. The government could not find the manager so they held John and his partner accountable. The courts put them both in jail. The court found that they were guilty of fraud. They did not steal the money or commit any fraud personally. As company directors the court held them accountable for negligence and failing to exercise due diligence. Due Diligence is exercising due care and attention to an important business issue (see Chapter 21 for more detail on performing a due diligence inspection when buying a business).

With the owners sitting in jail and the manager nowhere to be found the company was unable to sustain operations. You cannot win if you get kicked out of the game. Stop playing to win or lose. Manage and make decisions so that you are able to stay in the game.

Once I realized that my decisions would affect someone else's circumstances, I saw everything in a new light. No longer could I tell myself that "It does not matter. No one will fire me." What would happen if you approached every decision as if you were a steward? Personally, it woke me from a deep slumber of self-importance and an ego on steroids. No longer could I make decisions in the vacuum of my own thoughts. Now I enjoy clarity managing the business.

TIP

Operating as a steward is a higher standard of accountability. No longer will you view results as a win or a loss. You will find yourself thinking about what you can do to "stay in the game" instead of trying to win or lose. You will find yourself asking and answering questions like "Is this in the best interests of the business? What would my mother or father think of this decision?" It will simplify your life and ensure that you do not make decisions in the vacuum of your own thoughts.

If you think being in business is about "buying myself a job," or "something to do to make money," or "I want to be more independent," you are a little off track. Running a business has more to do with serving and "meeting the needs of a marketplace" than making money.

If your only reason to be in business is to make money, you will struggle to really make a good living. No business can flourish without a keen focus on meeting or exceeding the needs and expectations of a marketplace.

20. In general, I believe:
    a. Experimentation and testing is a normal part of business development. No one knows it all, and I prefer to figure it out as I go because I feel I accomplish more that way.
    b. There is nothing new under the sun. There is no need to change something just for the sake of change. If it is not broke, why fix it?
    c. Change, reengineering, and innovation are part of the normal research and development process.

Excessive experimentation can put you out of business. Unfortunately, this characteristic is also a leading cause of business insolvency. New business owners with little management experience are most guilty of taking experimentation to new levels of uselessness. It is tough to build momentum when the rules keep changing. It is even more difficult when the owner keeps changing the rules plus changes the game.

A growing business is a business in a state of flux. There is a need to shift and adjust to meet the pressure of increasing demand on the business resources. It is a healthy thing to innovate and make changes; just make sure that your people have the capacity to absorb the changes otherwise it will just create another crisis when people become confused.

21. Before making important business decisions I:
    a Ask staff, friends, or advisers for their opinion.
    b. Seek consensus with my team and then go with the majority.
    c. I decide what needs to be accomplished and then communicate my decision and expectations to staff.

Making major business decisions by seeking consensus is not a healthy business process. People tend to address major business decisions based upon their needs and agenda. They do not necessarily have the best interests of the business in mind when they share their opinions. Insecure staff might view it as an opportunity to tell you what you want to hear and thereby get closer to you.

Take the advice from people with a vested interest (staff, suppliers etc.) with a grain of salt. Ask appropriate questions based upon their experience and qualifications. Remember, they may be not be qualified to answer your questions and could even become overwhelmed by the question, feeling pressure to answer.

22. To determine a business to purchase I:
    a. Review financial statements to identify potential business problems.
    b. Ask the current business owner to identify and disclose potential risks.
    c. Read trade publications to get a sense of industry outlook and market conditions.
    d. Hire a consultant or third party to analyze the current situation and business outlook.

Buying a business should be more than a straight-line analysis of facts and data. Entrepreneurs are creating entire new industries and business opportunities ranging from ultraquiet motorcycle mufflers to roller blades. There are more than 20,000 different types of businesses to choose from. The sheer number of different business opportunities is expanding every year.

In order to locate successful businesses (many have not thought about selling), you will need to examine a wide array of sources. There are hundreds of things to consider when buying a business. You need to be intimately familiar with each and every one of them. Therefore it would be difficult to outsource this to a consultant. They will not have the same perspective as you nor can they be familiar with every industry or business.

Reading magazines and trade publications is a good way to get information about the business, but you need information about every aspect of the business and no one single source can provide all that information. You will get information from the seller, employees, publications, and your own experiences. But the best source of industry and competitive data is a salesman. Pretend to be a customer or a "secret shopper" and ask questions; you will be shocked how much they have to say and will tell you if you ask.

You cannot rely 100 percent on the business owner to disclose everything. Often it is not in his best interest to disclose certain information. All he is concerned with is selling the business. As flawed as that type of thinking is, it is true. Use the seller's answers as a base only. Seek out your own independent verification and information and then compare your own perspective to the answers provided by the owner.

23. My primary reason for wanting to buy a business is:
    a. I have extensive management experience and want to see what I can accomplish by owning my own business.
    b. I want to be more independent and have the freedom to make changes and decisions that I think will best meet the needs of customers and staff.

    c. To have a second career. I want to continue to be involved in a business during semiretirement.

    d. To grow my net worth. I figure owning a business I control and manage is safer than investing in the stock market.

    e. I have ideas, passion, and a vision for a specific industry and have identified a market segment that is not currently being served well.

    f. I have a product/concept that I want to develop, market, and sell.

    g. Owning a business has always been one of my dreams, and I feel I have something unique to offer.

    h. A business is the best vehicle to fulfill my ambition in life.

All of the eight answers to the question are good answers. Not everyone is cut out to be self-employed. It takes courage and a healthy ego to be self-employed. The fact that you got this far in this book says a lot about you. Does this guarantee success? No. But your willingness to read through this large list of questions shows a desire to learn. Without the desire to learn, you cannot grow. That is the genesis of courage: the willingness to grow.

There is definitely an adventurous appeal to owning a business, especially for men (we seem to have an adventure bug in our genes), and there is the temptation to jump right in. But it's important not to act first, then ask questions later. In fact I've heard it best described using an analogy of shooting a target. Some people fire, fire, fire, fire. Then eventually they say to themselves, "Uh, that did not work. Guess I better slow down and do this right. Ready, aim, fire." To be an accurate marksman you first aim at your target, ready yourself and the weapon, then pull the trigger to fire the gun.

TRAP

Getting excited and emotional about a business is important, but it does not supersede good planning and execution.

It takes courage to take the time to invest in planning before buying a business. It shows a healthy ego that is well managed, recognizes that you are not perfect, and that your time spent in this life is valuable and worth protecting.

There are as many good reasons to own a business as there are people. What matters is that you know *your* reasons and that they are part of a well thought out plan. Write down your reasons and the goals you wish to achieve being self-employed. Then weave them into your vision and mission statement.

24. I define business excellence as:
    a. Maximizing the amount of profit generated and meeting my personal goals.
    b. Controlling operations and making sure everyone is on track to meet his or her goals and objectives.
    c. Delivering a quality experience for each and every customer.
    d. I cannot succeed alone, and it is important to keep my staff and suppliers happy.

It is all about creating a quality customer experience. Restaurants provide some of the best and worst examples of what can be done to create a truly outstanding customer experience. A customer's service experience cannot be inventoried; it is experienced and there is no other factor that will directly impact the quality of a customer experience as much as the quality and passion employees demonstrate on the job.

Passion for delivering top-quality service cannot be trained. Quality can be managed and you can train people in the elements of service, but it is their personal passion or lack of it that makes the execution so substantially different. It is as individual as the person is unique. Their personal drive for excellence is what makes them overdeliver and strive to excel and please the customer.

It is not simply about hiring people pleasers. In fact it is the opposite. Hiring people who have an internal drive and passion for excellence that forms a personal code and pride that is pleasing to experience. Keep an eye out for people who overdeliver and really impress you. These are the people you want to recruit. They have that inner drive and personal standards that make them excellent employees. Plus they do not have to be managed nearly as much.

25. My long-term goal in owning a business is to:
    a. Build the business and then sell it to extract money to fund my retirement.
    b. Build a business that will endure for generations.
    c. Provide employment for my family and friends.
    d. Provide income during retirement or semiretirement.

A business can be an excellent tool to build assets for retirement and then extract them using a tax-advantaged strategy. An accountant or attorney that specializes in tax planning and counsel is your best investment if extracting cash from your corporation is your goal. It is important to structure your corporation to take advantage of these strategies. Depending on the state or province where you live, the strategies could vary somewhat so make sure you work with a local professional with experience in this area of corporate finance.

Providing employment for family and friends is a noble goal especially if you are a good manager and leader. If you are a control freak it may not work out well. I have seen family-run businesses do quite well. They are the exception, and typically their culture plays a big part in the management of the business. Often the matriarch or patriarch is the manager and the family members have worked in this situation from a very young age and control is not an issue; it is just the way things are.

To build a business for future generations will require a strong focus on building a culture that will endure after you are gone. You will have trained your successor to step into your shoes at the right time. Your business will need to serve a very wide spectrum of the market and have products that have a wide and deep adoption.

Buying a business to sell to use the cash for retirement can work, it is just risky. Your timing has to be perfect. If you look at the stock market, very few people can accurately time the market profitably. Flipping a business is influenced by the same factors that impact the stock market and is just as vulnerable. So unless you know something no one else does about the market, you will want to reconsider investing in a business just to flip it in a few years at a profit. It has been done but the risk is substantial.

26. The purpose of a business is to:
    a. Create profit and make me wealthy.
    b. Provide employment and help the community.
    c. Create customers.
    d. Increase goodwill in the community.

Once again, a business exists for one reason: to serve. When managed well a business will easily produce profits, but that result is secondary to the goal of having happy employees and customers.

Without happy employees, you will not have happy customers. How you choose to manage your business assets is what creates profit. But no matter what you do from a management perspective without happy employees and customers you will be spinning your wheels and wasting resources.

Plus when you have happy employees and customer goodwill is created in the community, it provides employment. Take time to verify if the employees are happy and determine the mood of customers. If they are both in bad shape, you will want to determine if this situation can be fixed or if it is too far gone to be worthy of your attention and investment.

27. In taking over ownership of a business I think it is most important to:
    a. Increase revenue.
    b. Increase the number of new customers.
    c. Increase the amount of business from existing customers.
    d. Increase profits.
    e. Add new products or services.
    f. Focus on creating an outstanding experience for customers and staff.

This is a trick question. If you increase the amount of business from existing customers by focusing on creating a great experience for customers and staff you will be profitable, get new customers, and increase revenue.

Focusing only on increasing the number of new customers may stretch your finite resources to the point that for every new customer that comes in the front door, one dissatisfied customer leaves through the back door. This is a losing proposition. Buying a business that has a high turnover of customers is a business that has not tried to control its growth. It may or may not be a good candidate to buy unless you are a really good manager who can put the processes and controls in place that the first owner could not or would not do.

28. The purpose of a manager is to:
    a. Motivate and cultivate staff thereby improving overall results.
    b. Control all operations, keep an eye on staff and prevent losses.
    c. Be a resource to teach, train, and modify staff behavior.
    d. Identify new business opportunities and markets.
    e. Be the center of the business operation and protect the owner's interests.

As a business grows and matures, the role of the owner changes and evolves. In the beginning it is important to be at the center of everything because you are the one and only employee. In growth mode the same trap can exist.

Avoiding being caught in the center of everything requires a self-motivated trained staff. They do not need to be told what to do because they are self-motivated. They are eager to improve and grow and make ideal candidates for internal promotions and advancement. As a manager you want your stable to be full of these thoroughbreds.

A mature business with solid staff and systems allows the owner to become the entrepreneur again. Your primary job shifts to looking for new business opportunities or markets that you can serve.

The stage of maturity of the business you are buying will have a big impact on what your role will need to be when you take it over. It will also be important to determine the role of the previous owner if that person is going to continue to help in the transition. You will now assume the management position of the previous owner, so it is very important that the previous owner have a role that is clearly defined.

29. When hiring staff, I look for:
     a. People with initiative, who can think on their feet.
     b. People that can get along with the existing team.
     c. Individuals with a solid education and a successful track record.
     d. Someone that fits the job description.
     e. A principled person with high personal standards and expectations.
     f. Someone who hates to lose and is highly competitive.
     g. An employee that demonstrates the creativity and tenacity to take on difficult assignments.
     h. A person with a strong work ethic over intelligence and experience.
     i. Staff members who can offset my weaknesses.

Simply filling a position because it is empty is not the right thing to do if it is the right person in the wrong seat. It will only create frustration for you and other staff. In a case like this you are better off waiting for a person who fits the job. If you run across someone with great skills and potential, you can always create a position for them, because they will make you money.

Each of the above answers if you put them together would be describing the ideal employee. Well that person does not exist. You might get three or four of those criteria when hiring someone, and as they grow in the job, you may witness these qualities coming forward. But do not expect that you can find the perfect employee. Sometimes all you need is someone with 80 percent of what you are looking for and you just learn to live without the other 20 percent; then when you do witness those qualities it is a bonus.

You need the staff on your side to make a successful transition, and after buying the business you will need their help. In fact, employees may be better sources of information than the seller.

Spend every moment the business is open with employees. Be kind and patient with them. They may be nervous even though the owner has given them permission to speak to you, or he may have given them other instructions as well. With the seller's permission, buy lunch for them once or twice during the process as a way to thank them for their cooperation. It will also be a good chance to get to know them better.

As you get to know the employees and the seller you will come to conclusions about each person, and they will be anxious to hear of your plans or to know how it is going. Tell them it is too early to tell. Take time to make good notes about each person and their comments.

Before you make decisions about their future roles, make a list of skills, abilities, and character traits you are looking for. Trust your instincts. You will likely never have the fresh perspective and insight as an outsider ever again. The value of this perspective is priceless. No adviser can replace your insight, observations, and opinions of the staff you have met and hopefully built relationships with.

Yes, you need people with initiative, who can get along with others and have a strong work ethic, but what other qualities are you looking for? What are your strengths and weaknesses? Make a list of what you are looking for and where you think gaps may exist that you will want to fill.

30. Working with a team of professional advisers is:
   a. Not very important.
   b. Somewhat important.
   c. Essential.

Professional advisers can protect your interests and help you achieve your goals. You need a team of advisers to help you take a close look at the business and examine what you are buying. For more information see Chapter 4.

PART 2

LOCATING A BUSINESS TO BUY

4
Working with Professional Advisers

The purpose of this chapter is to show you how to get the most from a team of advisers. Professional advisers protect your interests and help you achieve your goals.

To win in the game of football you need a good offense and defense. No one would go into a game of football without a defense because you cannot win if you only play the offensive half of the game. As ridiculous as this sounds, many businesses are so focused on the offensive part of their game (sales) they ignore protecting what they have with a proper defense.

TIP

In business your defensive strategy is made up of bookkeeping, legal, and management controls. Your defensive team members include management, bookkeeper, accountant, attorney, and you. Your business plan is a defensive tool that adds balance to your overall offensive and defensive strategy.

It takes both an offensive team (sales, marketing, advertising etc.) and a defensive team (administration, accounting, legal etc.) to win the game of business. No one builds a business alone; you should not buy a business alone. You need a team of advisers to help you take a close look at the business to make sure you know what it is you are buying.

The Team

Your team should be made up of a CPA (financial review) and an attorney (legal agreements, structuring the deal, etc.). You want to set a structure and put a fixed fee in place to define their roles and responsibilities and to tell them what your expectations are of them.

You Are Still the Decision Maker

Understand that the purpose of your attorney and CPA is to protect your interests. In a sense, part of their job description is to break your deal. They are looking for holes in the deal, liabilities that you should not be taking on. Their job is to help you identify potential problems.

As important as their role is, do not let them set your agenda, negotiate for you, or make decisions for you. Only you can do that, but you do want to ask them for specific advice. For example, if there are any environmental concerns, you will want to discuss any legal implications and issues that may need to be dealt with through the Environmental Protection Agency with your advisers.

Advisers Provide Perspective

You want your advisers to work with you to help you find potential errors, omissions, or problems on the seller's side. Their greatest value is that they do not have the same vested interest that you have; they are not buying the business themselves but helping you to buy a business. By working with them you get an independent third-party perspective. They have no emotional ties in the transaction and are free to speak from an unemotional perspective.

Often owners get emotionally attached to making a deal. When this happens, I recommend that you spend time working with your advisers. Ask them specific questions and ask for their opinion. Ultimately you will be making the decision, but their perspective could help balance your desire to make a deal with information and perspective you had not previously enjoyed.

Working with an Accountant or CPA

All accountants have a specialty. Some only do tax returns, others specialize in tax planning and financial planning, while others are experienced in dealing with corporations. If you can find a few with experience in mergers and acquisitions, that experience will be invaluable to you.

Your attorney's job is to help you prepare the legal agreements, including the nondisclosure agreement, letter of intent, and the formal offer. You should look for an attorney who is willing to offer you advice and to educate you about your legal obligations and fiduciary responsibilities. Especially if you are new to owning or purchasing a business, there are many specific things you will want to look at.

The Deal before the Deal

Professionals bill for their time and services by the hour, but you will want to find advisers that are prepared to negotiate fixed fees for the entire project. If they are experienced in this area of business, they should be able to estimate project fees pretty accurately. If they do not have direct experience, they will likely not be able to offer you a fixed fee because they do not know how much work is involved.

TRAP

Fees tend to escalate when you start to get into a formal offer. This is where a lot of changes and adjustments happen back and forth between your advisers and the seller's advisers. While this goes on, the clock is running and so are their fees.

It is amazing how quickly these fees can escalate the total cost of a project, especially if the seller asks for some specific changes and your lawyer does not like the wording. Then your lawyer has to make changes to the agreement and send it back to the seller's attorney; that lawyer has to review it, form an opinion, and then make a recommendation to his client. If the seller does not like it, they will send back another version and then your attorney will have to review it again—and he or she still has to explain it to you. I think you can see how all this communication between attorneys can create an escalation in fees that you had not anticipated. That is why it is so important to get a fixed fee for projects like this.

Business Brokers

Business brokers are business-savvy salespeople and only make money when they sell something, which is similar to the way real estate agents are paid. Instead of selling a building or property they are selling businesses.

Never lose sight of the fact that it is in the brokers' best interest to get you to buy because they only get paid when you buy a business they are promoting. I am not suggesting that business brokers are not ethical—in fact, in my experience they are quite professional—but you have to understand that the relationship between the seller and the broker is one-sided. They cannot really work in your favor; they have to work in the seller's best interest.

As long as you know that going into the relationship, it will help you to understand their perspective and what they want to accomplish. The more experienced the broker is the more savvy he or she will be and willing to work with you. It is a matter of screening and finding someone you are comfortable working with. As long as you remember that they are working for the seller, you will be in good shape.

Informal Advisers

You will also want to have at least one close and trusted friend who is willing to look you in the eye and tell you the truth or that you have lost perspective. You want someone in your corner who is looking out for your best interests and can provide a truly independent perspective.

Some business owners even go so far as to form an informal board of advisers. These advisers might range from other business owners to friends, family members, or other people that they respect who can contribute information and feedback from their depth of experience. As a result, you end up being much better prepared to deal with a particular situation. Plus, when you have to sit in front of a group of people who you trust and like to make a presentation, it really makes you think and it ensures that you're prepared. If you cannot convince your fans why you want to buy this business, why you think you need to make the deal, or why you want to make certain compromises to buy the business, you have a problem. If you cannot convince them or articulate your reasons with enough passion to sway them, you should probably not be pursuing the deal.

Your team of informal and professional advisers will help protect your interests and help you achieve your goals. That kind of support is always money well spent.

5

Finding a Business That Fits You

The purpose of this chapter is not to help you find businesses for sale, but rather to help you find a business that is worth buying. There is a substantial difference. A business that is worth buying is a business that must be in alignment with your skills, experience, and interests. Whereas finding businesses for sale is as easy as opening any major daily newspaper or searching the World Wide Web.

Businesses Are for Sale for a Reason

Buying a business is a lot of work, and if you are going to spend the time, effort, and energy to buy a business, it should be a business worthy of your time, effort, and energy. A business listed for sale in a newspaper is for sale because the owner wants out. This can happen for any number of reasons, including:

- Health concerns, retirement, partnership conflicts, and personal crises, including separation and divorce and the need to move to be closer to aging parents or family.

- Change in market trends, economics, and competition. Sometimes local bylaws make running a business difficult which has a negative impact on sales. Decline in local economy or crime in the area.

- Business has run out of cash, personal financial problems.
- Increased costs including insurance, legal, and litigation.
- Obsolete technology has eroded market position and ability to meet market needs.

There are lots of reasons that an owner becomes motivated to sell the business. It does not mean that the business is not a good candidate; however, a business dealing with the types of economic, market, or competitive factors listed above are in crisis. Business is challenging enough without having to deal with issues like local crime, local recession, or increased competition. It just makes sense that if you have a choice, look for a business that is vibrant and healthy.

Be patient. You will save yourself a lot of time by making sure you are selecting a good candidate in the first place. Remember, even after you make a decision on a business you want to buy, you still have to take time to build a relationship with the owner and the owner will need some time to put together all the paperwork and data for your analysis and due diligence.

TIP

You should plan to spend at least 30 to 60 days in the process of buying a business. In the beginning your progress will seem slow. You might feel frustrated, as if you are not making any progress. Just trust the process—you will get there sooner than you think.

Once you receive all the documentation and paperwork from the owner, you probably still have at least 30 days of work ahead of you. Make sure to give yourself enough time to do a thorough job and not be rushed into making a major decision.

Look for a Business That's Suitable for You

Personally, I would want to buy a business that is in sync with my personal preferences, life style, education, and experience. There will be less risk and potential for failure. After all, one of the major reasons to purchase an existing business is to reduce your risk. However, if you are not scared of risking failure, then purchasing a business you have no direct experience working in might be an option for you.

TRAP

Be cautious of relying on newspaper listings to locate potential business prospects. My opinion is that if someone has spent a long time building a business, they should be prepared to invest more time when selling it than what it takes to place a classified ad. Often these ads are placed to gauge interest or find out how much the business is worth. I do not know about you, but I do not want to be a guinea pig.

Selecting the Type of Business

Certain types of businesses will lend themselves to certain personality types and work experience. For example, a retail business located within a mall will have a lot of existing foot traffic and should not require a lot of advertising. In most cases, you will be making a contribution to the mall's advertising and marketing budget as a fixed fee or a percentage of your revenues. A retail operation is a good fit for someone who does not want to go out and try to find new business. However, there is a downside because you cannot just go out and grab people off the street to make them come to your store. You have to be patient and wait for them to come into the store.

On the other hand, in a business-to-business operation your sales team can go out and approach new customers and derive new business as a result. They can find customers you had never considered or known about. This type of business requires a strong sales team and management skills.

A manufacturing business will require a good understanding of the manufacturing process and perhaps engineering skills. Generally manufacturing businesses require a lot more working capital to purchase raw goods and production equipment than a typical retail or service business.

In businesses like construction, sometimes you are required to get a business license, and are required to prove that you have specific training in construction. Check the regulations in your area if you are looking at this type of business.

Service-based businesses are usually easy to start and run. This statement is based on the assumption that you can find the staff required to deliver your service.

Other options include transportation- or agriculture-based businesses. These businesses are similar to a manufacturing business in that they require larger amounts of capital to purchase equipment. In the transportation business, equipment can range from a taxi, courier, or delivery van to a long-haul 18 wheeler.

Consider Personal Interests and Hobbies

Depending on your age, you may find that a certain type of business has more appeal than another. Generally, the older we get the more conservative we need to be to protect our assets, retirement, and life style. Younger people do not need to take age into account because they have more time ahead of them, and they are therefore willing to put effort and energy into a business that carries more risk.

TIP

If you have interests or hobbies that you have direct experience in, this might be another option to consider in your search for a candidate. Just remember my warning from Chapter 2!

Perhaps you have a strong interest in environmental issues. It might be a good option to locate a business that is environmentally friendly or actually sells environmental products. It fits in with your value of making a difference in your community while allowing you to also make a living.

Consider the Business in Which You Work

Perhaps you have been thinking about purchasing the business where you are currently working. The advantage of purchasing this type of business is that you will likely have an intimate knowledge of its staff and structure, as well as the general health of the business and industry. While this might be considered a bold move, it is actually a sound strategy, especially if you like the business and its customers and the owner is getting close to retirement. The owner might welcome the opportunity to sell the business to an insider, but be aware that there is a risk that the owner might consider you a threat and fire you. I have seen it happen. Be cautious in approaching your boss.

Learn More about the Industry

Once you have an idea of the type of business you want to buy, it is time to learn as much as you can about the industry itself. It does not matter whether you have a lot of experience in the industry or none at all. The process is the same because the external factors affect everyone in the industry in the same way.

Look at the external factors in the industry your potential business is in. You should be looking at the big picture, not local market conditions (these will be covered in the market analysis section in Chapter 6). The goal is to better understand how the industry is performing on a regional, national, and international level. We are looking to identify trends, benchmark demand for products or services, and the general industry outlook for the next five years.

Once you find this data, you also want to identify and understand the barriers to entering the business and the growth outlook, including the impact of innovation and technology. In most cases it is also a good idea to examine the government's role relating to regulation, local zoning, and other community issues (crime, growth, decline, etc.)

You can find a lot of this information at Web sites like www.BizMiner.com, or you can also get the data you need from libraries, the Internet, business organizations, and trade associations.

Competitive Factors

Investigate the competitive factors involved in obtaining new customers. These issues include price, delivery, change, or evolution in products or services, and the reputation and image of the industry.

Is this a mature industry? Is it in decline or experiencing a fundamental restructuring? What is the size of the industry? Who holds the lion's share in the market? What percentage of market share do you need to acquire in order to achieve your business goals? What is the short-term and long-term outlook?

An emerging industry, while ripe with opportunity, may also present a significant risk. Factors indicating success may be difficult to identify because success has never before been achieved. Identifying your skill sets and planning for evolving the business will be the critical success factors. A *critical success factor* is a business practice, behavior, or attitude found to be present in every business that succeeds and not used by those that fail.

A mature industry poses a different challenge: Here it is much easier to identify factors that contribute to success, but major players tend to dominate the industry. Identifying the size of the market and the amount of market share required is the first checkpoint to determine the viability of the business you want to buy and key to determining your critical success factor.

If you are considering a business in an industry that is in decline or period of economic downturn, this presents a different set of issues. Opportunities may develop that would not normally be available. However, determining and confirming realistic assumptions of economic growth will be important because they will help support the assumptions made in your business plan. For example, what will it mean to your business plan assumptions if the economic indicators show an extended slump? On the other hand, if there is an indicator showing that the area is coming out of a slump and new economic growth is expected, the timing of your business acquisition would be a critical success factor.

An industry that is restructuring generally shrinks in market size. A good example is the recent changes in the oil and gas industry. Since the early 1990s the oil and gas industry has experienced substantial restructuring. Beginning in 1992, the oil and gas industry has seen marginal recovery in product demand and significantly improved profitability as a result of severe cost cutting (shrunk by 18 percent or $800 million since 1991, according to industry sources), rationalization of facilities, and downsizing. Your expertise, financial resources, and anticipation of opportunities may indicate great potential in this industry. However, investors and bankers may not agree, or at least not be comfortable with the volatility. You must prove that your assumptions and indicators are both accurate and attainable. That is why being able to quantify the factors driving industry growth or decline is so important.

Financial Health of the Industry

Revenue Canada produces an industry balance sheet. So does the IRS. This is an aggregated balance sheet that is compiled from corporate tax returns. It is an excellent tool to assess the financial health of the industry as well as to compare your financial projections and analyze your business assumptions.

For example, I conducted a comparison for one of my clients. We took his balance sheet and compared it to the Industry Balance Sheet. We discovered that his staff costs were almost 50 percent higher than industry averages. We also discovered that his profit margins were double that of industry averages. This tool can be a valuable and unbiased tool to test your business plan assumptions. Do your best to answer these questions:

What is the status of the industry?

How many new companies are opening?

What is the split in size (i.e., number of small vs. large companies and sales volumes)?

Which markets are being served well, and which are underserved? Which show the most potential for growth?

How aggressive are advertising and promotions strategies?

What are the value-added factors being used successfully?

How many substitute products or services are available?

Who holds the bargaining power, customers or suppliers?

How is the industry doing financially? Where do opportunities exist?

What is the status and reputation of the industry?

Customer Loyalties and Differentiation

What drives the loyalty factor in this industry? If industry competition is strong, how realistic is it that you can get customers to change buying patterns? Is being a "first mover" in an industry a help or hindrance?

Scale of Economy

How important is it to achieve specific production or volume levels? Keep in mind that the more you produce, the more efficient you become, which increases the amount of money you make per unit.

Cash-Flow Demands

A growing business can be in just as much of a crisis as a shrinking business because of the effect of cash shortfalls to pay suppliers and staff. The need to purchase large amounts of inventory will delay how long it takes to get a return on investment. If your industry demands carrying large amounts of accounts receivable, this may negatively impact your ability to pay suppliers and staff.

Staff and Delegation

If your service business relies heavily on skilled workers, how will your business attract the right people? What is the mid- to long-term outlook for skilled workers in your area? Are there adequate systems and information controls developed to provide an effective balance between delegation and control?

Other Things to Consider
Idea and Business Development

How will you develop new ideas? How will you balance your schedule to allow time to work on business development issues? After all, business moves at an accelerated pace today and no business idea lasts forever. Back in the 1960s a large company like Proctor & Gamble could count on a product life cycle of five to nine years. Today, they only assume a nine-month advantage. Access to offshore competitors has improved, and the new reality is that copycats proliferate quickly. A patent provides limited protection in international markets. How will you experiment and test new business ideas?

Diversification and Expansion

Changes in your marketplace and customer profiles may require you to let go of long-held cherished beliefs. There is always going to be a certain amount of imbalance between the marketplace and business strategy. The key is being able to identify the changes and make an objective decision on how you will adapt to changing market circumstances.

Specific Assets

The more specialized equipment and facilities you need the more difficult it may be to locate, repair, and if required liquidate quickly.

Fixed Costs and Contractual Agreements

Leases and financial commitments for equipment and facilities often survive the closure of a business. For a manufacturing organization the need to maintain a parts supply is often a legal if not a moral requirement. Other issues include agreements with labor unions, customers, and suppliers. What restrictions or impediments could there be to closing the business?

Government Regulations

Are there any existing, upcoming, or anticipated government regulations that could impact your ability to exit the business? List government regulations. If you are not aware of any, call your local chamber of commerce for access to government agencies.

Personal Values

Do you have a strong set of values or beliefs that will conflict with corporate or market values? List any personal conflicts that may arise.

Management and Emotional Factors

During times of economic change or crisis it may be necessary for the entrepreneur to shut down all or part of the business. Finding it difficult to do so might indicate an emotional attachment to employees or the business that could be unhealthy. What systems can you create to make sure that you make the right decision for the business and avoid attachment to employees and suppliers?

Relationships

Shutdown of the business may affect relationships with friends, suppliers, and other business units. Concern over maintaining image and identity may encroach on making a decision to close the business. Are your investors family or friends? If so, how will you deal with those relationships in case of a conflict?

6

Locating an Acquisition Target

Once you have determined the focus of your business search, it is time to shift from a strategic to a tactical approach to locate business acquisition targets. You can use a business broker or look in the newspapers or search on the Internet, but the best businesses never make it to the brokers and newspapers. These businesses are just silently sold. Therefore, a more intelligent and targeted approach is needed.

Create a Profile of Your Ideal Business Acquisition

In locating a business for acquisition you first need to identify the variables you will use to narrow your search. Here are a few examples of variables you could use to identify prospects:

1. *Location:* National, state, regional, city or neighborhood. If local, use zip codes to identify areas to focus on.
2. *Business Type:* Define the industry by Standard Industrial Classification (SIC) code, which classifies establishments by type of business activity.
3. *Demographics:* Number of employees, years in business, sales volume.
4. *Characteristics of the Seller:* Age, health or other life events that might cause them to consider selling the business.

5. *Price Range:* The amount you pay will have direct correlation to how long it will take to get a return on your investment.

6. *Financing:* Will you take advantage of seller financing, bank, or work with an investor?

This is a small sampling of variables that could be used to create a business acquisition profile. Edit this list to reflect a more accurate profile of the type of business you are locating. Put some serious time into defining exactly the type of business you are looking to acquire. The more specific your profile the easier it will be to screen out the quality candidates from a list. You will not be wasting your time kicking the tires (researching) and then test driving (meeting with the seller) because you know exactly what you are looking for. This also helps you recognize what you do *not* want.

Tapping Personal Relationships to Locate a Business

Assuming you want to purchase a business based upon your work history and experience, you will have contacts and resources you can draw upon to help locate a business that is for sale. You may have the name of some specific businesses in mind already.

If you do not already have the name of a business that you want to pursue, I recommend you contact major suppliers for their assistance and feedback. They could be some of your most valuable sources of information and competitive intelligence. They want to help you because they see you as a potential customer and hope to build a long-term relationship with you.

TIP

Tapping into personal resources should be your first choice. You cannot build a business by yourself. You will need to the help of many people throughout the lifetime of your business and having an informal team of advisers you can count on for information is a great way to build your own network. Plus, when you look at the circle of influence they have, you might just be able to find a good business candidate not previously considered.

Other sources for finding businesses that are for sale include attorneys, CPAs, industry associations, and even the chamber of commerce. Plan to attend industry events or chamber of commerce events in the area to meet other businesspeople and ask them for their help in locating a business to buy.

Try to meet the competitors' salespeople, posing as a customer to build a relationship and see if they talk enough for you to gather market information. They will tell you what they think if you ask specific questions and ask them what they think of certain businesses. They will tell you because they do not often get an opportunity to tell people what they think, so someone who listens to them and values their opinion is welcomed. Prepare some discrete questions in advance to get the ball rolling. Once the conversation starts they will keep the conversation going. Plus you get to see what type of people the competition is hiring to represent them.

Locating Businesses That Are Not for Sale

At any particular time there are over 20 million businesses operating in North America and 3.5 percent to 5 percent are for sale at any one time. The reality is that over the next 10 to 20 years there will be a number of baby boomers thinking about retirement. Businesses owned by baby boomers could make good acquisition targets. One of your strategies for locating potential prospects could include businesses within your geographic area where owners are 55 years or older. You can use personal contacts or even drop in and visit them to see if they are interested in selling their business.

No matter what type of business you are looking for, you want to utilize as many sources and leads as possible. If you only have one good prospect, you might feel compelled to compromise your requirements in an effort to make a deal. Whereas if you have a number of different leads in mind and one of them does not work out, simply move on to the next one and the next one. No one holds you hostage. You are the captain of your own ship.

TIP

Before you immediately go jumping into negotiations, slow down and the take time to think about who you are buying from. Gain an understanding of the type of people they are. Examine their reputation. Are they hard-working? Understaffed? Does the current owner live a conservative lifestyle? Or are they spending every dime the business makes?

Be prepared. The owner of the existing business may have different values than you. But just because they are different does not mean you should not buy the business. What this means is that while you are getting to know the owner you need to be careful about the value judgments you make. Plus understanding these differences will help you in your negotiations and in navigating the rough waters that may lie ahead.

Market Analysis

Study your local market to learn how it compares to the industry as a whole. Identify the current trends that are impacting the market and what new trends or changes will come into play over the next few years.

Then prepare an inventory of what you have learned about the local market and compare those results to the trends identified in the industry analysis. Once you identify the similarities and differences decide how this information will impact your approach to buying a business.

For example, if the local market is experiencing a downturn while the industry itself is regaining strength, determine how long it will be until the local market rebounds. Identify the trend, cause, and influences affecting the local market. If it is just a matter of a few months until the local market begins to recover, you should adjust your revenue and expense projections to reflect accordingly. On the other hand, if the downward trend looks to extend past a few months, talk to other local business owners and the local chamber of commerce to see if they have seen this before and determine how they view the next 12 months. If the local economy is going to be in a slump for the next 12 months, it is not a great time to buy a business. You would be better off waiting a year and let the current owner weather the storm or look for another business in a different market.

Competition Analysis

The goal of marketing is to clearly communicate your primary competitive advantage to your target audience, to find something that gives you a clear advantage over your competitors. To do that you need to compare your business to that of your direct competitors. If you had a chance to speak to your competition's salespeople, I am sure you will have picked up some good competitive intelligence.

Describe each of your direct, indirect, substitute, or potential competitors. Describe the differences, advantages, and weaknesses of your competitors. Create comparison charts that include an overview and analysis of the following:

- What do they do well?
- What do they say (in their advertising) is their primary competitive advantage?
- Identify their market share size, volume, and profitability. Are they bigger or smaller than the business you are looking at buying?
- Where are they weak? What could they improve upon?

- What are their characteristics, strategies, and operational methods? What price do they sell for? How would you describe the quality? Credit terms? Servicing? Sales and distribution methods? Reputation? Management background and expertise?

You can also acquire more information about your competitors from suppliers, customers, trade periodicals, company Web site, and their employees. You could also call or visit the competition to see how they perform or hire some friends and family to be "mystery shoppers." Ask them to buy something specific and then interview them afterwards to see what the experience was like.

Local industry trade shows are also a great place to visit the competition. It will give you a good idea how they present themselves to the public. The larger trade associations often publish reports and profiles of the industry and markets. If not, take the executive director out for lunch or coffee. He or she will see you as a potential member and will be open to your questions. Check out the advertising and marketing of your competitors.

Identify Trends in Sales and Profits by Market Segment

Every business has a variety of goods and services to offer to the marketplace. Some of those goods and services appeal to a specific type of customer. Depending on the makeup of the local market and your mix of products or services, you will sell more of certain items than of the less popular.

Identify how many products or services you will sell, to whom, and when. Then estimate the total sales and profits that will be generated by each group. Create a percentage breakdown of sales that each market segment will represent for overall revenue.

Not only will this information help you see where most of the profit is coming from, but you can also use this information to complete your sales forecast and cash-flow projections in your pro forma financial statements.

Market Size and Market Share

Market size and share answers this question: Can the market where your business is located support the business? Let's say your financial projections show that in order to be profitable you need a 20 percent market share and current market share is estimated at 13 percent. That would mean you would have to increase market share by 53 percent to be profitable.

Current Scenario	
Local population	50,000
Current number of customers	6,500
Current market share	13.00%
My Projections	
Local population	50,000
Current number of customers	6,500
New customers from market B	500
New customers from advertising	750
	7,750
Projected market share	15.50%

Figure 6-1   Simple Market Share Calculation

If the business you are looking at is in a mature industry, increasing market share to 20 percent from the current level of 13 percent would require stealing customers from competitors and finding new markets, while your competitor is trying to do the same thing. The battle for market share can be expensive and challenging. This scenario looks unrealistic and difficult to attain. On the other hand, if you adjust your entire operation to reduce expenses perhaps you would only need 15 percent market share to attain the level of profit required to be profitable.

Figure 6-1 illustrates a simple calculation that you can do using information that is easily accessible. Contact the local City Hall for the total population and ask the seller for the total number of customers served in one year. Simply divide the number of customers by the total population and that gives you your total current market share.

Then add new customers that could be gained from your new marketing and sales strategy and recalculate the numbers. In our illustration a small gain in new customers from increased advertising and tapping into an adjacent neighborhood would increase market share from 13 to 15.5 percent.

Local Market Information Online

I highly recommend the Web site www.BizMiner.com to obtain local market data. The prices are very reasonable and you can download the information immediately. It will save you a lot of time and energy trying to source out the information for free. Your time is valuable.

Importance of Estimating Market Share

Market share is a very important acid test when buying a business. Market share tells you how many customers you need from the local market to be profitable. If the market is too small or ultracompetitive, something will need to be done to increase the number of customers (increase market share) or else the business will not be sustainable in the long term.

The business you are looking at may have potential for gaining new market share, it may already have significant market share, or you may discover that carving out new market share could be difficult to achieve. Regardless, doing the research and a simple calculation can help you gauge whether a business is worth the asking price. Without that information you could end up paying too much to buy the business.

After all, this could be the reason the owner is selling. When a business is unable to attract enough customers (gain market share) to be profitable, something drastic needs to happen. You either have to move the business closer to your market, increase your advertising, or sell the business.

Market Area

You must choose your battles carefully. No business can sell to the whole world. Even an online business is going to sell products and services to people within a specific and definable market area. Customers in the closest proximity are the most cost-effective to service. You will also be able to better penetrate the markets that are closest to you. Determine which geographic area you will serve and try to identify new markets close by that you can tap into.

External Factors

The last issue to consider when looking at a market is to identify specific factors, trends, or issues that could impact sales performance.

For example, fluctuations in the customer buying cycle could negatively impact cash flow. What are the times of year that things tend to get quiet? Look at the seller's financial statements or build your projections based on your experience, on information gained from talking to competitors, or on information from an expert. Create a chart that shows the estimated peaks and valleys in your sales volumes.

If this information is not available, you could also seek help from other business owners who are no longer operating, former employees, and salespeople to get an indicator of any seasonal or local economic fluctuations in sales.

PART 3

DETERMINING THE VALUE OF A BUSINESS

7

The Goodwill Controversy

Goodwill is an intangible asset which gets its value from the business's good name, strategic location, high employee morale, and other factors that translate into above-average earning power. As a buyer, you may be asked to pay goodwill. The amount of goodwill can vary greatly from business to business.

Goodwill Is Subjective and Controversial

Goodwill is controversial in that people seem to think that if they pay goodwill, they have either paid too much or have been ripped off. This suggests that they have paid, or could pay, too much.

Determining how much goodwill to pay is a personal choice. It is also a business decision. The key is to make sure that if you invest your money, you know exactly what you are getting for it. As long as you can rationally justify the investment and you are reasonably sure you can get a return on your investment, all is well. You have not been ripped off. You simply made an informed decision that you are comfortable with.

Goodwill is not something you can hold in your hand or use, like equipment. Goodwill is intangible in nature. For example, to succeed in the retail business, location is important. If the business you are buying is located in a prime location, you can expect to pay extra to secure it. If the seller owns the property, you may be able to purchase it or lease it. If the traffic patterns are proven and the business is well known for that location, it will be money well spent.

Make sure you find out from the local City Hall if there are currently any development restrictions in place or if there any changes anticipated in the area. If the area continues to grow, it could be a strategic move to get the property. On the other hand if the area is in downtown, suburban sprawl will draw shoppers away from downtown.

The extra cost of a good location will be offset by a reduction in advertising and market expenditures because of the walk-in traffic. The opposite is also true. A bad location can become a real drain on cash reserves. Buying a business that is coping with a change in shopping patterns will be a challenge. No sense burdening yourself with a piece of real estate in a declining market.

Other intangibles you could be asked to pay for include reputation, brand name, management team, and the customer list. Any of these items can be valuable. It is a matter of how much you can afford to pay. A large, loyal customer list could be worth hundreds of thousands of dollars—money you do not need to spend in advertising and marketing to get customers.

Impact of Goodwill on the Price of a Business

Let us pretend that we have two companies in the same industry and each has the same amount of net assets (other than goodwill), which equals $100,000. See Figure 7-1.

Company A is an auto repair shop located downtown in an old warehouse in a hard-to-find cul-de-sac tucked away on a dead-end street. It has focused on marketing to people who drive in from the suburbs to work downtown, and it has been relatively successful. It has been in business for 15 years, is well run, but sales have slowly been dropping as residents migrate to suburban neighborhoods.

Company B is an auto repair and tire shop located in a relatively new suburban neighborhood on a main thoroughfare with high visibility. In business for just four years the business has been well known and popular since the neighborhood first opened. Prices are higher than those charged at Company A, but the owner provides free pickup and delivery of customers and their vehicles as well as a free car wash. They hold regular "Get to Know Your Car" events and seminars on a regular basis. The neighborhood is expected to continue to grow for at least the next 10 years.

The Buyer's Conclusion

In looking at both operations the buyer concluded that Company B is expected to have above-average earnings for a long period of time due to

1. Annual Expect Return

	Company A	Company B
Net assets (other than goodwill)	$100,000	$100,000
Normal rate of return in this industry	10.00%	10.00%
Normal return based on net assets	$10,000	$10,000
Expected net income	10,000	15,000
Expected annual above-average earnings	$0	$5,000

2. Buyer and Seller Goodwill Calculation

	Company A	Company B
Scenario A		
5 year expected above average-earnings (5 years × $5,000)	0	$25,000
Scenario B		
Earnings expected to be above average indefinitely ($5,000/10% = $50,000)	0	$50,000

3. Purchase Price Calculation

	Company A	Company B
Net assets (other than goodwill)	$100,000	$100,000
Total purchase price (net Assets + goodwill)		
Scenario A	$100,000	$125,000
Scenario B	$100,000	$150,000

Figure 7-1 Impact of Goodwill on Purchase Price

continued population growth and a superior location. Therefore, the business is expected to produce a rate of return above the industry average and therefore the buyer feels he is able to justify paying $50,000 in goodwill (see step 3 in Figure 7-1). Even when factoring in the higher purchase price, the combination of loyal customer base, marketing innovation, and brand recognition, Company B is a better deal overall due to its superior earning power.

My Conclusion

Company B could easily be found in any major city in North America. It shows that a retail-based business with a superior location, in a growing market is a superior investment for a number of reasons. The market outlook is positive for the foreseeable future, it has a long-term lease with an option to renew on a high-visibility main road, and the company enjoys a loyal customer base willing to pay above-average rates.

Company A has an average rate of return for its industry but struggles to maintain market share. The downturn of inner-city neighborhoods is affecting every major city in North America. These urban neighborhoods go through a painful restructuring that affects every business.

TIP

Even with aggressive marketing and advertising campaigns, it can be years before business activity levels return to inner-city neighborhoods. Businesses located in these areas, while healthy, do carry a higher overall risk, marketing, and management challenge.

Accountant's View of Goodwill

Accountants only record goodwill on a balance sheet when it is actually being paid, as in the above scenario when the business is purchased. This is to prevent information on financial statements from becoming too subjective.

If you ask CPAs how to calculate goodwill on a prospective business they would say that goodwill is a simple calculation that subtracts the fair market value of its total net assets from the company's net book value. However, that does not prevent someone from paying more than the amount from that calculation. The wisdom of paying goodwill is related to the estimated earning power of the business.

A Business Owner's View of Goodwill

Comparing the goodwill calculation in step 2 of Figure 7-1, Company B is a better acquisition candidate because its potential earning power is much greater than that of Company A. Company B has more exposure, opportunity, and potential to create and keep customers.

Therefore, the issue is not whether to pay for goodwill, but which business has better long-term prospects and can offer a superior return on investment. In this case Company B is the clear winner.

Every Successful Business Has Goodwill

Sellers often pad the price of the business by adding goodwill to the total purchase, which is equal to what they see as fair compensation for the future earning potential of the business. You can see from the example in Figure 7-1 that goodwill cannot always be justified. Just because the seller wants to get paid for the future value does not mean you should pay it.

TIP

Use the goodwill amount as a way to decide if you should buy, not how much you should pay. That is why it is so important to make sure that you locate more than one business prospect to investigate so that you have something to compare it to. That comparison brings a fresh perspective and clarity when making a decision.

Is the Price Inflated or Fair?

The best way to answer this question is to compare what it would take to start a business from scratch. It would take years to build a loyal customer list. Think about it. How long would it take to generate the same number of customers, supplier relationships, and trained staff? Plus an established business comes with confirmed cash flow. It takes time to build these things when starting from scratch.

From a simplistic viewpoint, a business is worth as much as a seller can get a buyer to pay for it. However, that is of little comfort and does not help you in making a decision to buy or not to buy.

Do the Math

Calculate how long it could take you, realistically, to build the same cash flow and profits. For example, if you buy a service business for $150,000, it could take as much as $1,000,000 in sales to generate that much net profit.

Have you ever sold a million dollars worth of anything? When I worked as a salesman in the automotive accessory after-market, I did $50,000 in the first two months, and in my second year I did $550,000. The next year was tougher due to an economic downturn. If someone was willing to sell me a business doing $1,000,000 in revenue for $150,000, I would buy it. Especially if I knew the business had healthy profit margins and a growing market, it would be an easy decision to make.

Whether you could get a business like that for $150,000 is another question. According to the Web site www.infousa.com there are 3,544,702 businesses in the major metropolitan cities in the USA with annual revenues between $500,000 and $2,500,000.

Creating Your Own Goodwill Up Front

Another way to deal with goodwill is for you to become an employee of the company you want to buy. Once you have created a substantial amount of goodwill, the seller converts your goodwill into shares, which gives you partial ownership. This can be a good option because the seller gets to maintain some control while you get your "legs" as a business owner.

You Can Pay Me Now or You Can Pay Me Later

I still remember the Fram Oil filter TV commercial that depicts a mechanic taking an engine apart. He extols the virtue of changing your oil and using a Fram filter because "You can pay me now or you can pay me later," says the mechanic.

TRAP

The most common reason people choose to start a business from scratch is to avoid paying for goodwill. They balk at the idea of paying for it. But my experience is that you will pay it one way or the other. You will either pay goodwill when buying a business or you will end up creating it for yourself. So either you pay the seller goodwill or you will create your own goodwill by putting in extra cash, time, and effort to develop a business with goodwill (more value than the assets indicate). Then you end up with a business with a bunch of goodwill and a need to extract that cash.

I hope you can see that there is no such thing as a free lunch—to get the cash you need out of the business you would need to sell the business to someone willing to pay goodwill to you!

Seller Financing

A way of dealing with goodwill is to get the seller to finance the purchase by accepting a personally guaranteed promissory note that is paid out of the profits the business generates after it is sold. This will give the seller a sense that he is extracting goodwill from future transactions, and you get a business with established cash flow that if you manage well, will pay for itself.

8

The Art of Business Valuation

Determining the value of a business is subjective, but there are common models and formulas used to assess the value of a business. Whether that number accurately reflects the true value of the business is a decision only you, the buyer, can make.

Value of Hard and Soft Assets

Making that decision involves looking not only at the numbers, which reflect hard assets, but also at soft or intangible assets. *Hard assets,* unlike soft assets, are things that can be easily identified, such as equipment, land, buildings, and inventory.

TIP

Soft or intangible assets are things like intellectual property, which are a result of intellectual effort. Patents, trademarks, designs, and copyrights are the main intellectual property rights. For example, a software development company has intellectual property wrought into the systems, processes, and programming that make the end product—the software—possible.

Another soft asset could be the management and employees that work for the business. Employees are often one of the most overlooked reasons to buy a business. Although intangible, it is the people that create additional value in a service-based business. You will not see them listed on a balance sheet as an asset, but staff can make a substantial difference in the results the business creates and therefore should carry a lot of weight in your decision.

The more that "service" is a key component of the business, the more valuable the soft asset. Since a service happens between two people, the experience cannot be pulled from the shelf like a product and has a direct impact on the perception of the quality of service. The reputation and ability of the staff to create a positive customer experience should be factored into how much you would be willing to pay for the business, especially if experienced people are difficult to find.

Acquiring experienced people in an industry with a shortage of good people could be a great reason to buy a business. In a competitive environment, the more specialized the required skill set is, the more challenging it can be to acquire key team members.

Value of Market Position

Market position and penetration take a great deal of time, effort, and resources. One way to expand your reach is to buy out a competitor. Access to exclusive products can be another important consideration. Distribution of unique products is often limited within a specific, exclusive geographic area. Buying a business that has an exclusive territory could be very beneficial for an existing business. You would be able to offer these exclusive products to your current customers and increase volume in your original business.

TIP

Significant efficiencies can also be gained by integrating two businesses into one business unit. Increased revenues as a result of access to exclusive products, consolidating inventories, and moving staff around can also increase efficiencies.

Evaluating How Much to Pay for a Business

As I have outlined above, how much a business is worth can be affected by many subjective factors. Depending on your goals and strategies, the importance you place on these factors will increase their value for business valuation purposes. From a practical perspective you should also subject the business to strict financial analysis.

There are a number of different methods to conduct a financial analysis, but they fall into three categories: industry comparisons, trend analysis, and asset valuations.

Industry Comparisons

An industry comparison is where the ratios of the firm in question are compared to industry averages. This analysis provides perspective on how the business is doing compared to its competition. Industry ratios are available from Dun & Bradstreet as well as online from resources like www.bizminer.com.

Trend Analysis

Trend analysis compares a business's present ratios with its past and anticipated future performance ratios and is often prepared by a CPA. This allows you to see if the company's financial condition is improving or deteriorating over a period of time. Trend analysis utilizes valuations based on the premise that the current value of a business is a function of the future value that an investor (or new owner) can expect to receive. It is the most widely used type of valuation and is generally used for valuing businesses that are expected to continue operations in the foreseeable future.

If you feel confident working with financial statements and spreadsheets, you might consider purchasing a software application called Cash Compass from www.paloalto.com. It will import financial statements from the most popular bookkeeping programs and allow you to make your own entries too. It will produce rock-solid pro forma financial projections to help you analyze trends and run various scenarios.

Asset Valuation Method

This analysis places a higher importance on assets, and therefore assets are the key metric used in determining the value of a business. All you do is add up the current value of all the assets and that is your price. While simple, it is not used that much. Not many sellers of a healthy "going concern" are going to be willing to settle for a price based on this calculation; only a business that is in distress may settle for it. Since a business is more than just assets on a balance sheet, you will also want to look at the earning potential of the business.

The proceeds from the sale of a business are taxable. In certain circumstances it may be in the seller's best interest to sell the business's assets as opposed to selling shares. Why? Because after taxes, they end up with more money in their pockets by selling the assets than they would by doing a share purchase/sale. If you run into this scenario, you will need to work with a good accountant to do a valuation and trend analysis to determine if purchasing the assets are in your best interest. For example, if you buy a business using a share purchase and the assets have already been written down for tax purposes, you will not get the tax advantages of depreciation on capital equipment. If you buy the assets outright you will be able to depreciate the cost of acquiring the assets on your financial statements. Speak with your accountant to get a deeper understanding of your particular situation before making a decision.

Common Valuation Methods

When your CPA completes the financial analysis of the business you are considering buying, he or she will discuss your plans and any problem areas identified in the analysis. This analysis and feedback from a professional will give you the facts you need to view the value of the business from a strict financial and accounting perspective. But if you are not an accounting or bookkeeping type, you may find it confusing.

What follows is an overview of the four most common methods used when placing a value on a business. You can use one method or a combination of methods to conduct a financial review and valuation.

Sales Multiple Method

The sales multiple evaluation is the easiest to understand. Let us say that you are looking at buying a business that has $170,000 in annual sales and $40,000 in net profits.

You multiply the annual sales of a business by a factor to arrive at the value. For example, annual sales × factor = selling price. A factor of 2 (a common factor used in some industries) in this example would be $170,000 × 2 = $340,000. When compared to an asking price of $225,000, this price looks acceptable. Read a little further and look at the same scenario using a different approach.

Earnings Multiple Method

With this approach we use the net earnings of the business to arrive at a value. So if you were selling a business using this approach, you would simply multiply the net earnings by a predetermined ratio or factor. If the net annual earnings are $40,000 and the owner has spent five years building the business, he or she may decide to use a multiple of five, which would make the selling price $200,000 (5 years × $40,000 = $200,000).

Since the owner figures that there will be some negotiating, he adds an additional $25,000 to pad the price and allow him some room to negotiate with a serious buyer.

Another way of looking at it is if the business had $40,000 in net earnings, it would take a little more than 5.5 years to recoup your investment assuming sales remained the same: $225,000 (asking price) divided by $40,000 (earnings) = 5.625 (multiple).

This earnings multiple approach uses a capitalization of earnings and places a value on the company's potential to earn money (profit). In this case it would take 5.5 years to recoup your investment. As long as you are prepared to tough it out for more than five years and there are no major changes in sales, expenses, and profit margins and you are comfortable with making a long-term commitment, this could be a good match for you. The real question is whether you see growth opportunities that you can use to increase sales and profits even further. Plus there may be an opportunity to negotiate down to $200,000 if it looks like the price has been padded.

It can be a challenge to come up with a capitalization ratio for a specific business. It is best to work with your CPA and do some research to find a ratio you feel comfortable with.

Discounted Cash-Flow Analysis Method

Using this approach you try to come up with a number today that will equal money you would expect to get in the future from the business. This method relies heavily on projected future earnings, whereas the capitalization of an earnings multiple is based on historical data.

Using the present value calculation you take the anticipated future net earnings over a period of time and discount that amount back using inflation and a reasonable rate of return.

Using our scenario of an asking price of $225,000, we anticipate that we could make a 6.90 percent rate of return and assume that inflation will run at 3 percent. If we use daily compounding and then calculate the present value of five years cash flow ($40,000), it would be just $137,125.47.

TIP

The discounted cash flow analysis method is a favorite with buyers because it is the most practical. It shows them what would happen if they did not buy the business, and simply invested their money and got a return of 6.90 percent plus 3 percent for inflation.

An argument could easily be made that the discounted cash-flow method to value a business is flawed because it relies on estimating future earnings. While true, only you really know how volatile the earning potential of your industry is and what local market conditions you will have to cope with. Valuation is an estimate. The accuracy of your assumptions determines the number. The real value of using the discounted cash flow with other valuation models is that it will generally produce a different number and provide a more realistic valuation. Looking at the business from many different perspectives (valuation models) is important because it helps you understand the value of the business you are buying and how much of a premium you are paying for the privilege.

Use Multiple Valuation Models

I think you can see that using different approaches in your analysis can provide you with different perspectives. Analysis is simply the value of a business expressed in numbers. The seller will have used some sort of valuation method to arrive at a selling price. If the seller has not had an independent valuation completed recently, your financial institution will require one. For a small business valuation, fees begin at $3,000 and can be as much as $10,000 or more. Note that financial institutions typically only use some variation of the asset valuation method because they are looking at the worst-case scenario, liquidation.

TIP

For the purposes of evaluating the value of a business you'd like to buy, you and your CPA will use either the sales multiple, earnings multiple, or the discounted cash-flow analysis method to make a value judgment.

However, no business is sold or purchased strictly based on the numbers. If there is a strong emotional position taken by one party, eventually someone will have to compromise in order to consummate a deal. The key is to do your analysis so that you are informed and understand the financial implications of making a decision to buy a particular business.

Other Considerations That Impact Value

In addition to the valuation methods we've discussed, you will want to see if the business has the ability to pay dividends. Dividends are taxed at lower tax rates, so using them to pay yourself would reduce the amount of taxes you would pay as a self-employed individual.

If the business has intangible assets, they will not usually show up on the financial statements as line items on an income statement. Depending on your business, local market conditions, and competitive factors, intangible assets could make a huge difference in the value of a business. Intangibles could include location, management systems, policies and procedures, market positioning, key staff, customer list, research and development, patents, trademarks, designs, and copyright.

A good exercise is to create a timeline of the business to document major achievements, milestones, and challenges the business has experienced. From inception to current date, what were the major milestones? Is this a business that is poised for growth or is it one that will need a lot of tender loving care to make it profitable?

TIP

The financial condition of the business can be a valuable asset. Compare the ratios of the business to those of the industry as a whole. Where does the business detour away from industry averages? Where does this business do a better job?

I remember an analysis I conducted for a client in the used machine tool business. I discovered that his gross profit margins were twice that of the competition, but he needed it because he carried twice as many staff too. Furthermore, because his prices were on the upper end of the market his inventory turnover was much less. So he needed the extra margin to pay for the extra costs of carrying inventory and making payroll.

How does the asking price for the business compare with the book value? Often the book value (i.e., assets – liabilities = book value) will be less than the asking price. The asking price is usually higher for a number of reasons including the current owner factoring in an amount for goodwill, barriers to entry (to read more, go to Chapter 12), and intangible assets.

What contracts is the company bound to and will those contracts survive a change of ownership? If so, they add value since you would not have to go out and negotiate your own. Plus if the product lines are exclusive, you would not be able to sell the product anyway so that could be another good reason to buy the business.

Check to see if there have been any prior sales of company stock. If so, this might indicate a previous attempt to sell the business where the owner ended up taking the business back. It could also indicate that the owner has done some advanced financial and tax-planning strategies or sold part of the company to get some working capital. In the latter case, the other shareholders would have to agree to the sale as well unless you want new business partners. Check with your CPA and attorney to see what the implications could be if you were to buy the business.

By checking with a business broker you might be able to compare the asking price to that of similar businesses, which will give you a sense of the market price. You can also hire a professional appraiser who will have a handle on the values for your industry. If you are serious about a business, the investment is money well spent and will help you when it comes time to get financing if you plan to use the assets of the business as collateral.

Understanding Appraisals

Assigning a specific appraised value on a business is neither right nor wrong. It is simply the best possible informed guess. There are several difficulties. First you have to rely on the knowledge and experience of the person performing the appraisal. The recent increase in the need for business valuation has strained the capacity of the industry. As a result, the average experience of those doing evaluations has decreased and in some cases the market segments are so new that experienced appraisers do not exist. An Internet-based business is an example of a business that is difficult to place a value on. Further, in order to come to a reasonably accurate valuation, the current owner would need to furnish supporting details that highlight the value of different elements of the business.

TRAP

When the valuation is complete the current owner could use the information from one or a series of evaluations to identify weaknesses and areas where the business value has been dropping. He may decide that he has enough information to fix the business and that he does not want to sell it to you. In addition, the owner could use the information from the appraisal to take corrective action to increase the asking price of the business. Be careful. You want to pay for the appraisal so you can keep it to yourself. If the seller pays for it, that could make it difficult to be certain that the valuation is unbiased and fair.

Appraisals can be used to identify where increased levels of investment could have a significant impact on the overall health of the business. This will help you as the buyer to see things from an independent third-party perspective.

Buying a business is a little bit of gambling, a lot of analysis, and building relationships. A strong relationship with the seller can keep the seller motivated long enough to allow you to make a deal.

Limitations of the Analysis Process

A limitation of trend analysis valuations is the time spent on organizing, evaluating, and verifying information from the accounting system that the business uses. The advantage of financial records is that they are unbiased but the weakness lies in the application of the accounting framework called *Generally Accepted Accounting Principles* (GAAP). Increasingly the value of today's companies lies in intangible assets which GAAP cannot adequately evaluate.

Appraisers will place a value on intangible assets such as skills of workers and management, intellectual property, business infrastructure, databases, and relationships with customers and suppliers. None of these are evaluated in accounting systems.

TIP

Tracking the value of intangible assets is critical with the increasing dominance of the service economy because the success of a business is increasingly determined by its ability to manage and deploy intangible assets. These assets produce inventions, which become new products or service innovations. Often these are more valuable than those measured by traditional accounting systems, which are designed to track only physical assets.

Currently there is no standard on how to evaluate intangible assets a business acquires. This deficiency is multiplied in high-technology companies where intangible assets are at the "core" of the business model.

The method you use to place value on a business will be different from what most banks and lending institutions use, which is book value when evaluating credit-worthiness.

If the bank perceives a higher than normal risk, it often uses the liquidation (asset) model to determine the value of a business. Banks and financial institutions are not interested in running a business if it fails. That is why banks use the asset liquidation approach, otherwise known as the worst-case scenario.

Valuation Is Not Absolute

Valuation represents what a company is worth to the buyers and sellers of a business. In reality, business valuation is a matter of supply and demand, and the business is worth as much as a buyer is willing to pay.

Whether you evaluate a business according to the value that a third-party appraiser provides or a business plan demonstrates, remember, it is at best a guess. It is a guess based on assumptions. How accurate your assumptions turn out to be, time will tell. In the real world, the valuation your CPA or appraiser puts on the business is more complex than a simple calculation on a spreadsheet. The actual value of a business is dependent on market conditions and your plans for the business. Your plans for the business can make all the difference in world.

9

Uncovering Hidden Assets: The Human Factor

Evaluating the employees of the business you are interested in buying is difficult, but important. You may not be able to do a full evaluation until you take over the business.

The Employee Information You Need

No list of information you need from the seller about the business's employees can meet the needs of every business or industry, because there can be unique situations depending on the industry and nature of the business. For example, if a lot of overnight travel is required of employees, you would want to know what policies are in place for compensation and managing the number of trips. Think about what you need to know, review the list below, and then create your own list. At the least, you should ask the seller for:

- A job description for each person, if they have one.

- Policies regarding compensation. You will want to find out if any commitments have been made regarding increases or changes in benefits.

- A complete list of employees, remuneration, benefits, and years of service. Ask the seller to identify those employees they consider "key" employees. Has the competition hired employees away recently? If so, ask the seller their perception of the circumstances and if the former employee has kept in touch with staff. Once word gets out that the business is for sale, competitors may try to hire other employees as well.

- The current status of the employee-employer relationship? Have there been any labor disputes?

- Ask the seller to share the reaction of the employees to the news that the business was for sale. Did any indicate that they would leave the company after the takeover? What were their concerns?

- Ask the seller to tell you what you should know that you have not asked about.

Be Cautious in Your Communications with Employees

Remember, at this point they do not work for you. Be cautious, humble, and professional. This is a challenging time for everyone involved. Employees may be wondering how your purchase of the business will affect them. You will sense tension, which is natural because they are anxious to know what is happening with their jobs. They may be curious, but you must resist the temptation to share confidential information. If you feel you must answer their questions, keep comments general and under no circumstances should you reveal specifics on negotiations.

Do not be tempted to take an employee or manager "into your confidence." It is not a good idea for a number of reasons:

- You may violate a confidentiality agreement that you have signed. This would be cause for the owner to terminate the relationship and take legal action against you.

- If you are unsuccessful in your bid to buy the business, speaking out of turn could disturb the relationship between the owner and the employees.

- At this stage, taking an employee into your confidence would be considered unprofessional and inappropriate conduct. It is your first chance to get to know them, and you do not want to be seen as unprofessional or to be setting a bad example.

Set Boundaries with the Owner

Obviously the seller will want to advise staff of his or her intentions to sell the business before they meet you. Come to an agreement with the seller as to what can and should be shared with employees.

Details regarding the deal, price, and timing are naturally confidential and off limits. Discussing your plans and ideas are safe territory, but do not disclose anything radical that might cause concern over somebody's job. It is too early to be making commitments, but you can leave employees with the impression that you are a person who is open to input and will listen to what they have to say. You might be surprised at what they have to say, and some of it could prove helpful in your negotiations.

I have been in situations where employees have mentioned that there have been a lot of staff layoffs, and they are nervous about their job, and they would be glad to see new management. This is a good news but also a point of concern to be followed up with the seller.

TIP

You will likely get questions about changes you plan. Some may be so bold as to ask what plans you have for them. Feel free to share personal values and communicate to them that you are a hard-working individual who values honesty and (insert your own values). Keep your comments general enough to leave the impression that everyone who can create results is safe. People do not like change.

Do not reveal any changes you might have planned for systems, people, computers, equipment, benefits, vacations, or remuneration. Should further clarification be required remain neutral and reiterate that you like to have people involved with decisions that might affect their jobs. This will display an open and sensitive posture that neither limits your plans nor disturbs the current business environment.

Get the Information You Need by Listening

You are not their employer yet, so you can use a passive strategy to learn more about the people you will be employing.

TIP

Since you will be hanging around the business gathering information there will be many opportunities to converse or observe conversations. These are ideal opportunities to gather information.

By remaining quiet, listening intently, and observing body language you can learn a lot. At first they will be careful around you and will be waiting for clues from you. You will need to be patient. Do not rely on first impressions. Once things settle down, everything will go back to normal, and opportunities to listen and observe what is really going on in the business will be revealed. Here are some questions to ask yourself as you observe the conversations and interactions between staff members.

- What is the subject of their discussion?
- What does this interaction tell you about the relationship between the employees? Is this simply a matter of different personality types or is there something deeper?
- Is there a difference of opinion? If so, do they understand each other? Who won the discussion? Why? Is there passive-aggressive behavior being displayed and by whom?
- Does this reveal character flaws in either person? Is this issue something management can solve? If there is a communication roadblock is it a structural or management issue or an attitude problem with employees?
- As far as customer interactions, are there any blatant mistakes or issues that you find unacceptable? Is the employee just having a bad day or could there be something else going on?

Before making firm decisions on staff, you first need to evaluate. Don't forget that once you take over the business you will see things change once again, especially between you and the employees. Remember, you probably saw them at their best when you were investigating the business. Once you take over the business and are officially in control, do not be surprised if behaviors you witnessed before have vanished, replaced by something else.

Pay Attention to Attitude

As you walk around the business, gathering information and meeting people, the beginnings of relationships are forming. This is a great opportunity to get to know employees and make fresh observations about their personality, character, and suitability. Make a spreadsheet with their names, position, salaries etc. Then leave a place where you can note your observations as well as those of the seller. Make notes about:

- How helpful were they and did their answers indicate a good foundation of knowledge about the subject?

- Did you observe any politics? Did anyone try to position himself or herself for the takeover? Are there cliques in the company?

- Do they enjoy the business and have the talent or skills that could help you build the business? Do they seem interested in helping you build the business? Did they share with you an area that could be improved or that they find frustrating?

- What were your initial impressions? Has that impression changed at all? If so, how specifically?

10

Selling the Seller— Gaining Cooperation

Beware of Your Comfort Zone

Buying a business is like a dance. You know you want to dance but you've got to have the courage and desire to actually ask someone to dance, or if someone asks you to the dance, to actually participate. Therein lies the biggest trap when buying a business: confidence or the lack thereof.

TIP

No one wants to look stupid and everyone is nervous. The seller is just as nervous as you, the buyer. The buyer wants to make friends with the seller, but the seller is going to be a bit distant until he decides whether or not he wants to take you to the dance.

Discard Fear, Be Confident

I have good news. You can be confident. Why? Just realize that you are in the middle of a process. Trust the process, trust your intuition, and ask lots of questions. You will be fine. There may be days when the seller is uncooperative. That is to be expected. It is a sign that you are on the right track.

Sure, that uncooperative attitude could be the seller's lovely personality showing or the fact that he is having a bad day. If you have been asking questions (as I have been nagging you to do), and suddenly the seller puts you off and does not cooperate, you have hit the mother load. There is a very good reason the seller is being evasive—you have touched a sensitive area. He could be feeling insecure or feeling remorse about selling. It may indicatate that he has changed his mind or it might just be remorse.

Bide your time. Questioning will uncover a sensitive area that he wants to leave covered up for his own reasons. That is exactly why you should feel confident. The system and the questions are working. Knowing you are onto something important is exciting. It is like someone walking up to you and handing you a thousand dollars—an unexpected but a nice surprise. Eventually it will become apparent what is behind the issue. If not, you will need to confront the change in the seller's attitude directly.

Free Money

So what would you do with a thousand dollars? When buying a business, touching sensitive areas and uncovering important facts is like getting free money. You have to ask yourself why the seller would not be willing cooperate in answering your question. Either the seller did not hear you, was distracted, or may have realized that you just uncovered the vulnerable spot and it bugs the seller, big time!

TIP

In cases like these, when you cannot get a straight or satisfactory answer to an important question, walk away. Let it lie a while, move on to something else. Wait for a better time to readdress the issue. If you are patient, there will be a day when the seller is in a better mood and the level of your rapport has grown. Ask again.

If there is still resistance you have two choices: Walk away from the deal, or confront it head-on and tell the seller that either you get the information you need or you walk. You have nothing to lose and everything to gain. Or do you?

Build Rapport

There is nothing in the world as powerful as having rapport. Rapport is a mutual understanding or trust and agreement between people. If you do not have rapport and trust you will achieve little in a relationship. On the other hand, strong rapport will increase your odds of making a deal.

Here are some rapport-building questions you can ask the seller:

1. What were their goals and dreams when they started the business?
2. How did it work out?
3. How did things change after a few years?
4. What are they most proud of?
5. What would they do different?
6. What has changed, if anything, since you started discussions and negotiations?

Use positive language. Avoid the use of negative language.

Negotiate, Do Not Demand

Remember, you are on the outside looking in. The seller may be feeling uncomfortable about selling the business, which is totally understandable. They spent years building the business, and now they have to let go of their "baby," and they are feeling remorse.

In sales, remorse happens after a transaction has taken place. When buying a business, remorse sets in when things start getting serious. It is a deep feeling of regret, or even grief. The seller begins to realize that their daily routine will change; they will no longer control the business, and someone else is going to benefit from their hard work.

It is your job to put them at ease and get them to cooperate with you. The key is negotiation.

TIP

Everybody negotiates. Children negotiate all the time. When they want something, they will come after you with every trick in the book. If they are really good at it, they will make you feel great while compromising. It is natural.

Some people are better at negotiations because they want it more, are better prepared, and will keep at it until they get what they want. When you are serious about what you want, the ability to negotiate will come naturally to you, just like it does to kids. When your desire is strong, your intent is true, and you keep coming at it from different angles, very few will be able to resist.

As long as you are negotiating for something that you really want, are sincere, and do not play mind games, you will get what you want. Just one thing remains. Get in alignment with sellers by listening for their needs, their agenda. There is something they want out of this deal, and you can help them identify what it is and help them get it.

It could be as simple as a concern over their son's future now that they are selling the business. Consider ways that you could help them help their son either by employing him or contracting out (to the son) something you need. If you needed a delivery service, why not ask if their son would be interested in starting a delivery service? If so, you could be his first customer.

Negotiation is the art of giving people what they want so you get what you need. You will read more about negotiation in Chapters 15 through18.

A Healthy Ego

Anybody that owns a successful business has to have a healthy ego or a great need for external affirmation. Ego can be an inflated sense of superiority over others, but it can also be a healthy awareness of your own identity and your skills and capabilities.

This observation on ego applies to you, the buyer, as well as to the seller. Two people with strong egos and self-confidence can make for a challenging engagement. You need staying power. Staying power comes from having rapport. Not flattery, but a genuine interest in other people and their point of view.

You reveal that you are interested in the seller by the types of questions you ask and how you ask them. I am not talking about a robotlike regurgitation from a list of questions from this book. Rather, a real interest in the seller's viewpoint. I am not suggesting that you have to agree with them, you just have to be genuinely interested and be willing to listen.

The Person Listening Controls the Conversation

Listening skills will trump eloquent speech and bravado when buying a business. The same is true in any important conversation. Think about it. When you are listening, you are able to make judgments, observe behavior, and prepare your next question. When you are talking, you are thinking about what you are saying, recalling memories, or making up something from scratch.

TRAP

Avoid talking too much. Sure, talkers can overwhelm you and eventually annoy you enough to give them what they want just get rid of them. But that is not someone anyone wants to have a relationship with. Especially in a business relationship, it is the person listening who is in control.

You maintain control by asking good questions that keep other people talking about themselves and in the process telling you what you need to know. People with large egos like to talk. Being confronted with a good question from someone they respect is conversational "honey"—sweet to taste and it never spoils.

Read Body Language

Body language is a mostly unconscious form of nonverbal communication. It is not absolute and should be used only as a supplement to arrive at conclusions and decisions.

If you become good at asking questions, you will have the time and attention to monitor the body and facial language of the people you are having a conversation with. You can use the nonverbal cues as an opportunity to continue to probe. You can even comment or probe about a particular expression. For example, "I noticed that when I mentioned reviewing the financial statements you began to frown and got very serious. What is that about?"

The more probing your questions the more you can expect to begin to notice body language cues. Often these cues can be an indicator of feeling uncomfortable or threatened or a sign of nonverbal disagreement.

A sudden shift in body position telegraphs an unspoken feeling, mood, or opinion. These cues are a strategic opportunity to probe deeper. You can form specific questions to get people to comment about their agenda, attitude, or uncertainties that may be marked by these nonverbal clues.

For example, turning away from a person during an important conversation is a way to show disagreement, rejection, and dislike. In the workplace this would be considered quite childish. But this behavior reveals itself in people doing other things while you are speaking with them. It can range from organizing their desk and work space to doodling on a notepad.

TIP

You can observe agreement or loyalty in a meeting by the way people align their bodies. If a number of people have their torso turned toward one person at a conference table this shows respect and a visual cue as to the power that person holds.

Eye Contact

The greatest resource for body language is the face and eyes. Emotions range from showing feelings of agreement, to anger and uncertainty. The range of nonverbal emotions that can be observed in the eyes and face are wide and varied.

Eye contact rarely lasts longer than a few seconds before one or both parties experience a strong urge to look away. Breaking eye contact has the effect of lowering stress levels.

On the other hand, someone who locks onto your eyes might be trying to conceal something. In espionage, when an agent is surprised, they are trained to maintain eye contact to avoid looking shifty-eyed. By maintaining eye contact all the other person notices is the eyes, taking the attention off what they were doing.

TIP

Rapid blinking of the eyelids is a fairly reliable sign of emotional stress, triggering the fight or flight response.

Generally, we begin a conversation by looking away and end it by looking back at the listener. While speaking, we alternate between gazing at and gazing away. Obviously, the more direct eye contact the more people like each other. There is less eye contact when people disagree or dislike each other.

Facial Expressions

Changes in the chin, lip, brow or cheek muscles of the face reveal emotions, opinions, and moods. These nonverbal cues must be used with caution, but they can be good indicators of true feelings and hidden attitudes. Remember that many facial expressions, like a smile, have been shaped by culture, personal experiences, and implied business etiquette and rules.

Understanding the Seller

Knowing the strengths, weaknesses, and needs of the seller will help you gain an understanding of that person's agenda and priorities.

Realize Everyone Has Weaknesses

Every personal weakness of a business owner ends up being reflected in the business itself. You will need to clean up these areas of the business that have been impacted by the weaknesses of the seller.

When you spot a weakness, hold your tongue. All you can do is cope with the weakness. The nature of your relationship does not allow you the opportunity to provide feedback, make observations, or change them. In fact it could cause your deal to terminate because business owners do not like to be criticized much at the best of times and certainly not when they are thinking about selling their "baby" to you.

Observe, Take Notes

You should, however, make notes of these weaknesses. Use this information to frame your approach to reviewing financial statements, operations, and staff. Unless the business has a really good bookkeeper or accountant who deciphers sloppy records, you can be fairly certain the financial statements will likely not reveal much detail. In this case you will need to ask the seller lots of questions to unravel the financial history.

Another common weakness in many business owners is mismanagement of human resources. Be prepared for everything from staff with a high turnover to a team of people who are working together but whose relationships are highly dysfunctional and dramatic. Human resource issues can be expensive and time-consuming to resolve, which can make it especially difficult for the new owner.

Remember, when you take over the business you are not a social worker or counselor. If staff members are resistant to changing their behavior, you may have no choice but to replace them. Starting to replace staff can also have the positive side effect of motivating other staff to clean up their act.

Make sure that your plan reflects strategies to deal with the weaknesses you have identified.

Understand It Is Their Baby

Every business owner I have met is proud of his or her business. Whether it is a one-person home business or a multinational business, every owner has a sense of pride and accomplishment. Owners will defend and protect their baby. Do not put yourself in a position where they feel the need to protect it from you.

PART 4

HOW TO MINIMIZE YOUR RISK

11

Show Me the Money

Understanding Financial Statements

Sellers know how to read their financial statements and without a working knowledge, you are at a distinct disadvantage. Reading financial statements are a basic business skill that no one considering purchasing a business should be without.

TIP

Invest time in reading this chapter and then enroll in an introductory accounting course at your local college. Every business college has evening programs that will provide you with a basic working knowledge, and you can ask questions about the stuff you do not understand.

Following the Money Trail

Financial statements are like a trail of breadcrumbs that will teach you everything you want to know about a business. This chapter will not turn you into an accountant, but you will be able to carry on a conversation with the seller, your accountant, and attorney. If you cannot read the financial statements provided by the seller, you will not have a complete picture of the business.

Without a basic understanding of what financial statements contain, you will be dependent on professional advisers. You will still need an accountant, but with the basics you can carry on a conversation and ask intelligent questions. You are the business owner—or soon will be—and many financial decisions will have to be made. Having a rudimentary understanding of business financials will help you get started.

Financial statements will provide you with a lot of information. Over time you will learn more and more about the meaning and implications of certain items on a financial statement. Everyone starts out knowing little or nothing about reading financial statements, but with a basic understanding your learning curve will increase dramatically and so will your confidence.

Introduction to Financial Statements

A corporation is a separate entity from its owners. It has all the rights of an individual except the ability to vote. Financial statements provide a structured and universal format to display assets, income, expenses, and debts of a company to allow a third person to assess the corporation's financial health (i.e., when considering lending money or buying a business).

This chapter contains definitions, examples, and information to help you not feel quite so overwhelmed and to enable you to carry on a conversation with your accountant.

The Five Types of Financial Statements

There are four basic financial statements used in accounting. The fifth, known as a *pro forma financial statement*, contains projections in the same format as the four types of statements that accountants use. Each financial statement will cover the same time period.

Income Statement

The income statement reports results of a company's business operations (revenue and expenses) for a set period, usually one year or one month. It shows whether the company earned a profit or not. Net income is earned if revenue exceeds expenses. A net loss is incurred when expenses exceed revenue. The statement lists the amount and types of revenue and expenses.

The income statement may also be referred to as an *earnings report, statement of earnings, statement of operations,* or *statement of profit and loss.* Figure 11-l shows a basic income statement.

Statement of Changes in Owner's Equity

The statement of changes in owner's equity, as the name implies, shows information about what happened to equity during a period. Owner's equity is an important part of the balance sheet. You will find the equity entry from the statement of changes in owner's equity on the liabilities side of the balance sheet listed as Owner's Equity, Stockholders' Equity, or Retained Earnings. Figure 11-2 shows a basic statement of changes in owner's equity.

Balance Sheet

A balance sheet shows the net worth of the company. The balance sheet shows you what you own minus what you owe on a specific date. It is based on the calculation

Assets – liabilities = net worth.

The balance sheet may also be called a *statement of financial position.* Please note that in the sample balance sheet in Figure 11-3 both sides of the sheet are equal. This is the reason it is called a balance sheet. The name also

Smith Sales, Inc
Statement of Income
For the Year Ended December 31, 2004

Revenue from Sales		$300,000
Expenses		
Cost of goods sold	$230,000	
Selling expenses	30,700	
General and administrative expenses	28,200	
Income taxes expense	1,700	
Total Expenses		$290,600
Net Income		$9,400

Figure 11-1 Sample Income Statement

Sam Company
Statement of Changes in Owner's Equity
For the Year Ended December 31, 2004

Sam Company Capital, November 30, 2004		0
PLUS		
Investments by Owner	$ 9,000	
Net Income	$ 1,600	
Total		$ 10,600
LESS, Withdrawals by Owner		$ 4,000
Sam Company Capital, December 31, 2004		$ 6,600

Figure 11-2 Sample Statement of Changes in Owner's Equity

reflects that it reports the balances of assets, liabilities, and equity at a specific point in time. It is a close cousin to a personal net worth statement except that it is a statement for a business.

Statement of Changes in Financial Position

The statement of changes in financial position will show how much cash was on hand at the beginning of the period and how much cash was left at the end. It shows where the money came from and where it was spent. See Figure 11-4. It provides the key ingredient to good cash management: what you spent, where you spent it, and whether your cash position increased or decreased.

Financial statements reveal everything that went on in a business at a particular point in time and are a snapshot of the business situation on that particular day.

Pro Forma Financial Statements

Pro forma financial statements are hypothetical projections of future performance for a business. They follow the same format and structure as official financial statements and include a balance sheet, income statement, and cash flow analysis. They are based on a set of assumptions that estimate what may result in the future from actions in the present. These assumptions will

Benny Sales Inc.
Balance Sheet
　31-Dec-04

Assets		**Liabilities**	
Cash	$ 1,100	Accounts payable	$ 960
Office equipment	$ 7,200		
Telephone equipment	$ 1,600	**Owner's Equity**	
		Benny Jar - capital	$ 8,940
Total Assets	$ 9,900	Total Liabilities and Owner's Equity	$ 9,900

Figure 11-3　Sample Balance Sheet

include revenue, expenses, and expected profits. Pro forma statements are used in business plans, loan requests, and earnings reports. They estimate how the financial position of the company will turn out if certain assumptions are achieved.

Retained Earnings, Stockholders' Equity

Any successful business will have retained earnings. These are the profits that a company has earned during its existence. Often business owners prefer to keep earnings within the company as retained earnings. Then they pay out the retained earnings to themselves and shareholders as dividends, which are taxed at a lower rate than taking the income as salary.

Stockholders' equity is calculated by adding common stock plus preferred stock plus retained earnings.

Another way of calculating stockholders' equity is by subtracting total liabilities from total assets. This is sometimes called *net worth* or *book value*. If the seller has included a lot of intangible assets in arriving at his asking price, goodwill could substantially exceed the total of retained earnings and assets.

Other small business owners prefer to "zero out" their corporate earnings each year by having their accountant estimate how much of a year-end bonus they would need to pay themselves in order to "zero out" the corporate earnings. In cases like these you will not see a lot of retained earnings in the company. Rather you will see dividends or bonuses paid out each year.

If you need to make a comparison with industry averages, simply add up the dividends and bonuses to come up with a rough number of what the retained earnings would be if they had not been zeroed out in the books each year.

EZ-Bread Company
Statement of Changes in Financial Position
For the Year Ended December 31, 2004

Cash flows from operating activities

Net Income   60,000

Adjustments to reconcile net income to
net cash provided by operating activities

Increase in accounts receivable	$ (20,000)	
Increase in inventory	$ (13,000)	
Increase in prepaid expenses	$ (2,000)	
Decrease in accounts payable	$ (5,000)	
Increase in income taxes	$ 5,000	
Loss on sales of shop assets	$ 3,200	

Total adjustments $ (31,800)

Net Cash Provided by Operating Activities $ 28,200

Cash Flows from Financing Activities

Cash received from issuance of shares $ 15,000
Cash paid for dividends $ (14,000)

Net Cash Used in Financing Activities $ 1,000

Net increase in cash $ 29,200
Cash balance at beginning of 2004 $ 8,000

Cash balance at end of 2004 $ 37,200

Figure 11-4 Sample Statement of Changes in Financial Position

Goodwill

Goodwill, as discussed in Chapter 7, is an intangible asset that exists when a business is valued at more than the fair market value of its net assets. It is usually due to strategic location, reputation, good customer relations, brand name, management team, customer base, or similar factors. Good will is equal to the excess of the purchase price over the fair market value (FMV) of the net assets purchased.

Cash-Flow Analysis

Cash-flow analysis calculates cash surplus and shortfalls. They are projections based on past operating experience and include payment of obligations and collection of receivables. Cash-flow forecasts provide a fundamental financial-management tool for planning cash needs and ensuring adequate liquidity.

Fair Market Value

Fair market value is an amount at which property would change hands between a willing buyer and a willing seller, neither being under compulsion to buy or sell and both having reasonable knowledge of the relevant facts.

Fair market value would not apply in situations when a business or its assets is sold at rates below fair market value. Obviously, if you make a deal on a business that is in distress, you may be able to build the business up and sell it at fair market value and a profit.

Liability Accounts

Accounts Payable

Accounts payable is money owed to others for goods, supplies, or services purchased on open account on behalf of the business. Accounts payable transactions tend to have a time lag between the receipt of services or the acquisition of assets and the payment for them. Each purchase is recorded separately to track what is owed and when the obligation is paid. You will find the period of credit on most invoices. For example: 2/10 means take a 2 percent discount if paid within 10 days. N/30 means payment is due 30 days from date of invoice, and EOM, or end of month, often becomes 30 to 60 days.

Total Liabilities

Total liabilities are all the claims against the assets, debts, and obligations owed by a business to its creditors. It is calculated as total assets minus total equity.

Cost of Goods Sold

Cost of goods sold or cost of sales, as the phrase implies, documents the cost components of a product or service that is sold to a customer. In a manufacturing scenario the cost of goods sold embodies resources used (i.e., the raw materials, labor, and factory overhead required) to produce the product. For a service business, cost of goods sold would be based on the direct labor components of that service. For example, in a repair garage, wages paid to the mechanics are a cost of sales, as are the parts used to repair the vehicles.

Current Liabilities

This is a balance sheet item that equals the sum of all money owed by a company and due within the current fiscal year. It can also be called *payables* or *current debt*.

Long-Term Liabilities

Long-term liabilities will not come due for payment within the fiscal year. These can include business loans, long-term notes due to shareholders as well as any mortgages that will become payable.

Check to see if these long-term liabilities can be assumed by you. In other words, can you take over the payments and what kind of guarantee or security will you need to provide?

Asset Accounts
Accounts Receivable

As an asset account, accounts receivable records cash owed to the business arising from the sale of goods or services to customers. These are sales made on credit. Sales can be services, goods, or equipment. Each transaction must record the amount owed to the business as well as payments received from the customer.

Are customers paying invoices on time? What are the trends? Is there a time of year when customers do not pay according to terms?

Current Assets

Current assets are the cash, accounts receivable, marketable securities, and inventory. Combined, they make up the total of the company's current assets.

Paid-In Capital

Paid-in capital is the amount paid for the stock sold by the business. For example, when the business starts, cash is placed in a bank account to allow the business to operate. This cash is exchanged for an equal value of company stock. You could also see this account when a partner buys into the business.

Intangible Assets

As discussed in Chapter 8, intangible assets are long-term assets used in a business that lack physical substance. Examples include patents, copyrights, trademarks, and franchises. In the case of a company that develops and sells software, patents or copyrights are what have value for you as a buyer. The software without the patent or copyright is just software you can use. You have no rights to change, modify, or resell it.

Proprietary secrets, systems, and formulas should be protected by signed nondisclosure agreements from all staff. Ask to see the signed copies of the nondisclosure agreements to make sure they are current or even exist.

TIP

Find an attorney experienced in intellectual property. They work with this stuff daily and are worth the extra investment if your purchase involves patents, copyrights, trademarks, or franchises.

Total Assets

Total assets are a company's total current assets plus total fixed assets. Long-term assets include property, plant and equipment, and other fixed receivables and investments. Total assets can be found on a company's balance sheet.

Fixed Assets

This is a long-term, tangible asset used in the business. Examples of a fixed asset include equipment and real estate that is not expected to be converted to cash in the current or upcoming fiscal year.

Depreciation

Depreciation is a cost of an asset over a period of time for accounting and tax purposes. Over the years this account will show a decline in the value of the property due to general wear and tear or obsolescence. This is the opposite of appreciation.

Accumulated Depreciation

This is an account used to keep track of the total depreciation recorded on a specific asset since acquisition. It is used to record an accumulation of the credits made to track the expiration of and estimated life cycle of the fixed asset.

Net Profit

This is a company's total revenue less total expenses. This shows what the company earned (or lost, called *net loss*) for the period, usually one year or one month. This is often cited as the "bottom line" on the income statement. It is also called *net earnings* and *net income*.

Gross Profit

Gross profit is a simple calculation. Subtract cost of goods sold from total revenue to get gross profit. Gross profit is often expressed as a percentage of revenue.

Net Worth

Net worth is calculated by subtracting total liabilities from total assets. It is also called *owner's equity* or *shareholders' equity* or *net assets*. Sometimes people refer to it as the *book value*.

Appraisal

An appraisal is an estimate of the value of a property on a given date determined by a qualified professional appraiser. The value may be based on replacement cost, sales of comparable properties, or the property's ability to produce income.

Financial Analysis

Financial analysis can take many forms. It can include benefit-cost analysis, life-cycle-cost analysis, and cash-flow analysis. I like to use a version of a cash-flow analysis called a *sensitivity analysis* to see the impact changes in a company's costs and fluctuations in revenues would have.

Business Plan

As discussed in earlier chapters, the business plan describes a business's objectives, strategies, market, and financial goals, as well as the organization's current status and plans for the next three to five years. It projects future opportunities for the organization and maps the financial, operations, marketing, and organizational strategies that will enable the organization to achieve its goals.

Generally Accepted Accounting Principles (GAAP)

GAAP is a formal set of accounting principles, standards, and procedures used by accounting professionals. It is a combination of authoritative standards set by standard-setting bodies, as well as accepted ways of doing accounting.

Professional Financial Advice

With increased costs for E&O (errors and omissions) insurance, professionals are careful about providing advice. So at best the advice they will give is hedged, with an extra helping of caution for good measure. In many respects the advice they provide is often antientrepreneurial. Whether you are starting, buying, or running a business, risk is always present. Often professionals' advice is couched in terms to protect them from lawsuits.

TIP

When you get advice, take it to heart and consider the implications of what you were told. Ask for tips on how to interpret and view certain information. What does it mean? Ask them what you should be thinking about. It is unrealistic to expect much more of professionals than the preparation of documents and delivery of technical services.

12

Prepare or Repair

Create an Acquisition Plan

An acquisition plan is a type of business plan focused on the unique issues in buying a business, especially one that involves purchasing the shares or stock of a business. The purpose of committing your acquisition plan to paper is to look ahead and plan how you will go about assuming or taking possession of the business in question. A good acquisition plan will have the following sections:

1. The Acquisition Target
2. Your Business Goals
3. Operational Information
4. Legal Structure
5. Products and/or Services
6. Industry Analysis (see Chapter 6)
7. Marketing Strategy
8. Operations
9. Implementation Plan
10. Financial Plan (see Chapters 13 and 14)

This chapter covers all the above sections of the acquisition plan except those covered in the chapters indicated in parentheses.

The Acquisition Target

Business History

Write one paragraph that documents the history of the business including the legal name, type of corporate entity (i.e., C-Corp, S-Corp, LP or LLC), directors or shareholders. Include any specific information you have about the business and the seller.

TIP

If you know the annual revenues, profits, and asking price make sure to include that information.

Why It Is for Sale

There could be a hundred different reasons that a business can be put up for sale. It's important that you document why you think this business is for sale. For example, a business might be for sale due to deterioration in the health of the seller. Another reason could be that the owner wants to retire and needs to sell in order to fund retirement.

Opportunity

In the beginning you are looking at the business from the outside, but now you've begun to look from the inside; this provides you with a fresh perspective. That makes this an ideal time to commit your ideas to paper.

Tell the reader of your acquisition plan what makes this business a favorable candidate and describe the current situation. This will either be the easiest or toughest part of your acquisition plan to write because it is the most important. If you cannot make a compelling argument about your reasons to buy this business, you need to go back to the drawing board.

TIP

Spend as much time as needed thinking about the business and what opportunity you see so that you can clearly articulate the opportunity, your vision, and your plan for buying this business.

It is quite common to wait until you have everything else complete before attempting to write this section. New issues, ideas, and opportunities will come to your attention as you work on the other parts of your acquisition plan.

It should not take a whole page to explain the opportunity. It should be no more than one or two paragraphs. If you feel that the business has untapped capacity or expect that you can increase efficiency (and profits) say so, briefly. You can provide all the details in the plan.

Current Condition of Assets

Provide a brief summary of the condition of the assets including the building, equipment, and strength of the business. Is the equipment in good working order? Will any of it need to be replaced or refurbished? State the appraised value and how much capital will be needed for new equipment.

TIP

If the building needs renovations to implement your plan include a brief summary of the renovations, why they are needed, and how much the renovations will cost.

Market Position

A well-established business with a large, loyal customer base will have a strong market position. Although intangible, this asset can be quite valuable. The degree of value will be determined by how many customers you can keep following the transition.

Impact of Change in Ownership

There will always be some customers who have a strong relationship with the seller. When a business changes hands customer relationships change, too, and customers could modify their buying habits. Therefore, you must factor that into your revenue projections. Spell out exactly what type of impact the change in ownership could have on sales.

Timing

Your notes here can be as brief as stating the expected acquisition date. If your time frame is short, it is very important to communicate the exact timeline, seller expectations, and reasons for the short timeline.

If you are financing through a bank you cannot expect the bank to fit into your timeline unless you have been preapproved or have been feeding them information about the deal. Ask them how long it will take them to make a decision on financing.

TIP

A stock purchase is more complicated and likely to take longer than an asset purchase.

It is important to understand the legal implications and differences between an asset purchase and a stock purchase. With an asset purchase you are simply buying the assets. The advantage of an asset purchase is that you buy the assets and set up your own operation without any of the liabilities from the other business. With a stock purchase you are actually purchasing the company from the previous owner and assume all the liabilities and assets. The upside is that you can simply continue operations exactly where they were. The downside is that you assume all the liabilities known or unknown from the previous owner. It is important to make sure that you and your advisers have examined the business deeply enough that you understand the implications of your purchase.

Your Business Goals

Identify the goals and objectives of the business by explaining, as specifically as possible, what you want to achieve. Most goals can be expressed as numbers: e.g., sales, percentage income by product or service group, expected return on investments. Other legitimate goals can include:

- Provide better quality service
- Fast delivery
- Reduce costs, etc.

Your goals can be general, but they should be measurable. Start with your personal goals. Then list your business goals. Examine both to assure that they are in alignment. Compare them to your vision and mission statement. Are they in alignment and complimentary? If not, rework and remove the conflicts.

TIP

Create two sets of goals: short term and long term. Short-term goals can range from 6 to 12 months while long-range goals can be 2 to 5 years. Create a list of goals with a brief description of action items. Since you are buying an existing business, you should put an emphasis on your short-term goals. You should include important milestones, including notifying customers of the change of ownership, special marketing campaigns, and staff meetings.

Allow yourself a period of adjustment and allow extra time for customer communications, meeting with suppliers and staff.

Operational Information

Provide a schedule of the hours the business will be open. Identify key employees, including a description of their abilities that make them vital to the success of the business. You may decide to devote a separate section to employees if you think they are key to your success. Identify the number and type of employees and the organizational structure (attach a table showing who is responsible for what).

Legal Structure

This is the place to document the date and the business structure (proprietorship, partnership, or corporation). Also, identify any anticipated changes, i.e., initiating a partnership, taking on new shareholders.

Products or Services

The next step is to write a description of what your business will sell. The tendency is to gloss over this section, as it may seem obvious to you. This is usually due to the degree of familiarity and knowledge you have.

Remember, the purpose of the acquisition plan is to demonstrate the ability of the business to deliver goods or services and to gain the confidence of the reader, i.e., banker, investor, or the seller in the case of an owner-financed situation.

TRAP

Avoid skipping or cutting this section short. Consider the readers. They do not have your experience, knowledge, or desire. Focus on providing enough information to accomplish two objectives: to gain the confidence and trust of the reader of your acquisition plan. Demonstrate that you know how to run your business and achieve your goals and objectives.

Anticipate what the people reading your plan might be looking for: e.g., a banker will be interested in financial projections. A seasoned businessman might be more concerned about your commitment, skills, and the business concept or viability. Modify and edit the plan for each specific group. Provide them with enough information to answer any questions they have as they read your plan. Avoid writing needless detail. Provide just enough information to answer their questions and gain their confidence. The purpose is to set the stage for a meeting and educate the reader about the important elements and key success factors for your business.

Start with a clear and simple statement of what your product is or what service your business will provide. Avoid the temptation to compare your offering to similar services or products. Reserve that for the competitive and marketing analysis. Focus on what makes your offering unique and preferable to customers. Explain what it does, how it works, how long it lasts, what options are available, and any proprietary rights, etc.

TIP

Of particular importance is whether you are planning to make any changes in the product or service offerings. Be sure to describe the requirements for any associated products or services (especially vital for software, e.g., computer).

Another issue to consider is whether you hope to sell items on a one-time or infrequent basis, or if repeat sales are your goal. If you are buying a retail store, bakery, or restaurant, you are going to count on the same customers returning on a regular basis. What percentage of customers do you expect as repeat customers? What has been the experience of the previous owner? Explain if your projections differ and why that is important to the business.

The description should include:

- Description of the line of products and services: What are the services, uses and characteristics? How are the products used? What are their features? What makes them unique?
- Mix of products and services: What is the collection of the various services and products offered by your business?
- Depth and breadth: List the number and type of products or services offered. Identify the depth and breadth of individual services and products. Will you provide a narrow or broad mix? Why? Remember, 80 percent of your revenues will come from 20 percent of your products or services. The more you are able to identify the 20 percent with the best margins, the best possible acceptance by your customers, the greater your chance of success.
- Positioning: how well known is the service? Is it well accepted by customers? Is it a planned or unplanned expense?

Be cautious; try not to be everything to everyone. There is a fine line between diversity and distraction. How much profit will this mix of products or services add to your bottom line. For example, sales of a particular item might make up 25 percent of your projected revenue. However, it only contributes 5 percent share to your total net profit and adds 35 percent to the cost of delivering your product or service. Focus on the services or products that create 80 percent of your profits.

Plans for Expansion

As the business grows, requirements change. New staff may be hired; new facilities, equipment, and tools are required. Identify the items, costs, and time lines and make note of them.

Costs and Profits on Services

Describe each of the individual services, revenue, and cost components and profit margins. Can you identify the time required to prepare, manage and create the service yourself? Multiply your time by what you would have to pay to have the service performed by someone with your level of experience, education, and reputation. Remember, add the cost of any materials used directly in the project.

Costs and Profits on Products

Identify the line of products you plan to sell. Describe the costs and profit margins. If profit margins vary between product lines, create a list of the product lines and show the specific profit margins.

Expansion or Redesign of Services or Products

Describe the evolution or staging of your services or products over the next three years. In service businesses, the time available and reputation of the service provider can limit the scope of the business.

Identify products or services that can be expanded to grow the company. Timing is an issue. Be realistic about the time it will take to develop the business systems and evolve services. Timing issues are also reflected in financial projections and affect the marketing strategy. Remember, record any associated costs on a separate worksheet.

Change in Costs and Profits

What changes in your costs and profits will occur over the next three years? What are the factors that will influence costs and profits? Will you be able to achieve any economies of scale, increase in market share or profits?

TIP

Think beyond the transition phase. How will you reduce costs, improve productivity, or handle simultaneous projects?

What about business momentum? As the company's reputation grows with an aggressive marketing, sales, and promotional campaign, the business should be able to attract more customers. If the business has little or no competition, the business may attract competition and reduce its market share in the second and third years.

Service or Product Life Cycle

Every product or service has a life cycle. Is it a fad, trend, or choice? Are these new and emerging trends or are they relatively mature? Some trends have been around for years and may become obsolete or simply lose market share over time. Write a brief overview of the history of your service and changes you anticipate over the next few years. Approximate time lines:

Fad: Lasts less than 2 years.

Trend: 2 to 10 years.

Lifestyle choice: 10 years plus. These get absorbed into the culture or community.

Every product or service goes through a series of phases: introduction, growth, maturity, decline. The length of time it takes to go through each phase varies. Fads go through all phases in less than two years. Other services and products may be pushed ahead by technology and innovation.

Customer Profile

Here you will identify each target market group and identify the distinguishing characteristics, i.e., demographic, psychographics, and behavior variables.

You might have many "customers" that have input into the decision process. Each of them needs to be identified, categorized, and understood. Determining your customer profile will require undertaking a complete market segment analysis to identify each group. Then choose the most desirable groups or those with the greatest potential. Are you selling to the end user or is there a middle man? If there is a middle man, then you will need to do two profiles: one for the end user and one for the middle man.

Customer Preferences

Remember the definition of marketing: It is the process by which information about a product or service designed to meet a need—real or otherwise—is communicated to those who have the need. The process may take place on the spur of the moment or it may be planned. However, the goal is always the same: To get people to consider the merits of whatever is being sold.

Try to imagine yourself as being employed by your customers. If they are your boss, you will let them tell you what they want to buy, how they want it, how much they are willing to pay, as well as where and when they want it provided. They will also tell you what else they expect for their money.

Remember, look for the biggest bulge of buyers for your specific product or service and then package your product or service to meet their needs head on! Your strategy is to position your business at the same level as the majority of the buyers. It is critical to figure out where the business is positioned in the marketplace plus your plans for any changes you have in mind.

To accomplish this, you need to understand your customer and be able to put yourself in your customers' shoes. Today, customers have good crap detectors, and they are looking to do business with companies that understand their needs, wants, emotions, and perceptions.

The concept then is to direct all your company resources toward your best prospects. To communicate in such a way that all your communications vehicles (brochures, Web site, logo, ads, etc.) clearly mirror your targeted audiences' most wanted needs and desires in your product or service.

Product or Service Attributes

Describe the different attributes of each service and how it adds value for each target market. To some degree the demographics, psychographics, and geographics of your primary, secondary, and tertiary segments will dictate their preferences for a specific product or service. In the markets you have chosen, what do customers want? Less stress? To save money? To experience a smooth transition on move-in day? More safety? Simplicity? Some information on preferences will come from the industry analysis. Some of it must come from speaking directly with your potential customers.

Proprietary Rights

Describe any legal means you might have to protect your services from use by your competitors. Describe any special skills or abilities you have that give you a competitive advantage, even though that is not protected by law or contractual agreement. Do you have special skills or knowledge that is not easily obtainable by the competition?

Industry Analysis

Chapter 6 provides all the information you need to do a thorough industry analysis. Refer to this chapter and then include your findings in your acquisition plan here.

Marketing Strategy
Marketing Tools

When marketing is done well, the prospect will be motivated to investigate further or acquire the item or service. Accomplishing this objective will involve the use of numerous tools and strategies. These include brochures, post cards, business cards, newsletters, Web site, telemarketing campaign, direct mail, advertising, networking, press releases, books, and e-zines.

Marketing Strategies

What will your marketing strategies be? Some things to consider when working on marketing strategies are:

Location

Customer proximity to your business

Proximity of your primary competitors

Distribution methods: i.e., wholesale, retail, manufacturers agents, strategic alliances

Credit policies

Product and service guarantee and warranty

Sales model

Pricing strategies

Special events

This, by no means, is an exhaustive list. The important principle is this: Get your message to where the customer is! If you are in business and interested customers do not know your product or service even exists, you might as well close the doors! Marketing is the process of finding and getting access to your primary market.

For example, I recently saw an advertisement for a company promoting specially prepared foods and snacks for diabetics. The commercial ended with the line: "available at your local drug store." I have to admit that initially I thought, huh? Then I got it: where do diabetics go to get insulin? The answer, a drug store! Absolutely brilliant.

Here's another example: a customer once told me about one of his suppliers who used a unique approach to promoting their products. This company sold wood waterproofing sealers. You use this product on any wood surface to protect it and seal it from water damage. The strategy—they have a full-time meteorologist on staff. Why? As they studied the market they discovered that people are more predisposed to purchasing the product after big rainstorms. So they hired the meteorologist to provide them with weather forecasts to help them schedule advertising campaigns!

TIP

Get creative. The role of marketing is to get your message to as many motivated prospects as possible.

Pricing Decisions and Strategy

If there is one issue that will kill a marketing or advertising campaign it is not having a well-defined market pricing strategy. This strategy is central to the overall development of a successful marketing strategy. Price objections can kill your business. Generally, the less personal interaction you will have with a customer the more accurate you need to be about your pricing strategy.

Remember, marketing is communicating the benefits of a product or service. If your price is too high or low, your prospects or customers may not take you seriously or dismiss your proposition outright. The entire purpose of marketing is to communicate and create a perception of value! Choosing the correct price is essential to creating the right perception of value.

Create a Market Price Strategy

Market price strategy is the art of balancing the role of price as a means to attracting customers and keeping customers.

Every price creates a perception of value in the mind of your prospect or customer. The goal is to find the fine line between a price that is low and unsustainable versus too high, which handicaps the marketing and sales process. A price that's too high or low can still create a perception problem. Overpriced products or services do not have enough value in the mind of the customer. A price that is too low could create the perception that the product or service is of poor quality. The point is this—both scenarios create a perception problem. An effective market price strategy strikes a balance between real perceived value and the maximum sustainable price for goods and services for a particular market segment.

A market price strategy that works well in one market segment may fail in another. Do not assume, research your competitors pricing strategy, test your own with real live customers and then adjust to fit the market.

Pricing your product or service to achieve maximum profits and market share is a delicate balance. The problem is that most companies do not have a market price strategy or policy. Ignore this important marketing principle at your own peril.

For example, if your price is too high, you may not be able to achieve enough market share and lose important sales and profits. If your price is too low you may be leaving money on the table, and you will not have enough profit to sustain your operations. The solution? Find a balance between these three factors (see Figure 12-1).

To establish your market price strategy, you will need to consider the following points:

1. Determine an acceptable range of prices in accordance with your corporate values and objectives. Do you want to establish a discount image, or a quality image? The key is to make sure that your decision is in keeping with your corporate values.

2. Set a target price for a specific target market. Based upon your understanding of this market and the estimated demand, you next set a price that will maximize sales and profits.

3. Estimate the demand. Compared to your competitors will your price bring you enough market share? If the share is too small, either adjust the value in the proposition or select a new price.

4. Try to determine competitors' reaction. If your price and expected share generate enough volume, you will want to anticipate your competitors' reaction. If your price is too low, a price war could break out. If your price is too high, it might stimulate a new competitor with a lower price.

Figure 12-1 Finding the Right Price

5. Compare and test the price against your financial goals. Can you meet an acceptable level of return on your investment or will the payback period be too long? It is best to test your price against your financial needs and goals as early as possible.

6. Is your price congruent? The price must be evaluated based upon a number of factors, such as comparable products or services, distribution channel, advertising expenses, and any personal selling strategies that will be used.

7. Develop a profit plan. Create a spreadsheet that looks at the cost of production plus the cost of marketing and distribution at the anticipated sales levels. A lack of profit will require establishing a new price or finding ways to reduce costs or add value.

Finally, set your final price. Take into account the price of competing products or services and adjust your price to fit. For example, a price of $91.56 may have been established but the final price may be $89.95 for psychological reasons. If you plan to use a high price-skimming strategy you may want to be ready to anticipate lowering prices so that market share does not dip significantly. Generally speaking, the more mature your industry the more aggressive you may need to be in your pricing strategy.

Operations

Define how communication takes place. Who reports to whom? Provide an overview of job descriptions, titles, and duties. If you have a number of staff, a flow chart can easily communicate the structure and reporting lines.

Key Management and Staff

The smaller the organization the more important this section becomes. Other than the financial section of your business plan, this section is the next most important to an investor or banker. They need to be able to answer the question: Can this person run this business? Do they have a reasonable chance of achieving their goals? You want to show that you have access to a group of advisers or professionals to help you grow your business and make decisions.

Provide a brief overview of any key staff and management. List their qualifications, experience, and brief job description. Put a detailed version of the job description in the appendix.

TIP

Do not forget yourself! Include a personal resume for each key management and staff member.

Decision Making and Business Development

Your business plan is based on certain assumptions. Some of these assumptions will prove to be correct and others will not. The key in any successful enterprise is the ability to learn and then quickly apply that new knowledge.

This will require making certain strategic and tactical decisions to ensure your success. You want to provide an overview of your decision-making process.

Getting outside, independent feedback will help offset the risk of making decisions, omissions, and expensive errors. You might get feedback from staff, customers, or suppliers.

Have outside consultants ready to review important decisions and make suggestions. Anything that helps you objectively assess your current position and future direction of the business will greatly increase your odds of success.

Implementation Plan

A well-thought-out implementation plan will make you nothing but money. The trick is to think ahead to the implementation phase while you are writing the acquisition plan. Decide how you will actually implement and use all the ideas, concepts and strategies identified in your acquisition plan. After all, if it was important enough to write into the plan it is important enough to track, manage, and implement. Perhaps this seems obvious. Yet, I have personally witnessed well-intentioned entrepreneurs short-circuit themselves by not implementing, testing, or executing a well-thought-out strategy.

It is very easy to get distracted and forget about the commitments you made in your acquisition plan. There are two ways to prevent this from happening:

1. Reread your business plan and compare how you are doing.
2. Create a separate implementation plan. I like to use a calendar format. I like to assign deadlines, priorities, and people to the implementation plan.

Essentially, you want to integrate your business plan into the way you work. If you put a timeline to the tasks and then decide to delay or postpone doing the task, at least, you made a conscious decision. If you do not hold yourself accountable by assigning who, what, and when to your priorities, they can be easily forgotten.

An implementation plan has three periods:

First 30 days following takeover

60 to 90 days after transition

The first year

Identify the tools required to promote the business: brochure, Web site, press release, direct mail or e-mail, etc. Then identify the systems and strategies, including staff training, human resource systems, and customer service, to name just a few. The important thing is to identify, develop, and then implement them.

Financial Plan

Your financial plan will show the financial history of the business, revenue forecasts, expense budget, and profits. See Chapter 13 and 14 for details on writing your financial plan.

13
Business Finance

Financial Information You Need to Organize

Before your accountant can work on financial projections, you need to gather and organize the raw financial information to pass on to him or her. The documents needed include a list of assets (an appraisal may also be required), inventory, and the last three years of financial statements.

Sales Forecast

Compile a spreadsheet of monthly expenses for the first year and annually for the second and third year for all products and services. Past financial statements could be a big help. Ask for the last three years of financial statements from the seller.

Direct Cost of Sales

These are the direct costs of items associated with manufacturing or producing the product or service. Items will include raw materials, labor, sales expenses, and so on.

Operating Expenses

Include sales and marketing payroll for all sales and marketing employees. If sales commissions are paid, make sure to include them too.

Sales and marketing expenses should include travel, entertainment, and promotions like tradeshows and other events.

Advertising and promotion expenses include all advertising, printing, and promotion expenses.

General and administrative expenses include your payroll for your office and administrative staff. Make sure to include an amount for payroll burden, including employers' portion of Federal tax, workers' compensation, insurance (liability, disability, group, health), depreciation, leased equipment, utilities (gas, electric, water, waste disposal), rent, office supplies, telephone, cell phone, Internet access, and contract consultants.

Other Common Expenses

If applicable you should look for association dues, automobile expenses, bank service charges, merchant credit card charges, other employee benefits, and equipment rental. Make sure to include an amount for interest expense, finance charges, as well as licenses and permits that might be required. Do not forget about yourself and your draw or salary.

Your Accountant's Functions

Your account is responsible for reviewing financial statements provided by the seller to determine compliance with local, state, and Federal tax laws and remittances. Your accountant is also responsible for the preparation of your pro forma financial statements.

Unless you have a lot of accounting experience, you should outsource preparation of pro forma financial statements to your accountant. He or she will prepare the pro forma financial statements according to Generally Accepted Accounting Principles (GAAP). This format will allow you to make comparisons between your projections and the financials provided by the seller.

The pro forma financial statements are the best test for the viability of the business acquisition and will be used by investors and bankers to make a decision. Without them you force the bank or investor to do their own financial projections.

Financial Projections

Financial projections are created toward the end of the process to document all costs associated with your business and acquisition plan. Make notes of costs and planned expenditures as you are discussing them with the seller. This will save you time when starting on building your financial plan.

Do not short shrift this part of the process. The best way to sabotage yourself is to try and bluff your way through your financial projections. Do not be tempted. Take the time to thoroughly prepare yourself and the people who may be reading your plan by documenting your revenues and costs.

Your Financial Plan

Writing your financial plan is a two-step process. Start with documenting your income and expense assumptions. This is where you detail item by item and month by month the costs and revenues associated with starting and running your business. When complete, you take your spreadsheet of income and expenses to an accountant or CPA to assist you with the development of your cash-flow projections.

A Word about Projections and Forecasts

All too often I have witnessed new owners taking over a business only to be surprised that revenue fell short of their expectations. Unfortunately, they counted on sales remaining the same and had no plan. If you are organized and very focused, you might not experience a substantial drop in revenues. From a conservative point of view you should expect that revenue would shift downward somewhat in the first three to six months. This can be prevented by taking the time to plan ahead for the transition and making sure you stay focused and keep your staff focused.

The Purpose of Financial Projections

A forecast quickly becomes obsolete. So why bother? The purpose of the forecast is not to make a perfect projection of what will happen but to go through the exercise of examining how you will manage money based on specific assumptions you have made.

By the time you decide to draft a financial plan, the planning process has probably been going on for quite some time, even if it is just in your head. Many portions of the plan will be derived from the analysis you performed as you thought about your idea. Nevertheless, assembling the written financial plan is more than an exercise in translating your thoughts to a printed page. It is testing the financial viability of your ideas and business operation. The discipline of creating financial projections will either validate your plan or expose its vulnerabilities.

TIP

When your projections do not show the levels of profit you thought, do not just add more to the revenue side to inflate profits. Examine what would need to change to produce those extra profits. This is the secret of business planning. It will serve you well to look for the underlying issues of why profits were not as high as you anticipated. If you can identify a realistic approach to increasing revenues and profits, you have a great opportunity. If not, you can walk away. Hold yourself to a higher standard.

Gather Historical Information

When preparing a plan for an existing firm, financial and operating information developed over the company's life will be absolutely essential. Past financial statements contain the historical information that will provide most of what you need for a written plan; they include:

- Bookkeeping and accounting records, i.e., financial statements
- Customer purchase history and supplier information
- Tax returns, employee payroll records, and personnel files
- Cash-flow projections from previous plans, spreadsheets, and other planning documents

Most owners have developed a feel for how the company is doing. Remember, this is subjective and should only play a part in your planning. For example, you may feel that you are not being compensated at a level that is appropriate to the amount of time you put in. A plan that calls for you to continue working long hours must establish that, in your mind, the benefits derived from implementing the plan are worth the effort.

TIP

If you are simply buying a business in the same line of products or services as your former employer, what you learned as an employee may be right on the mark for your new company.

Financial Planning Tools

If you are committed to a do-it-yourself approach when creating your financial plan, then you should seriously consider purchasing Business Plan Pro

can find links to Business Plan Pro on my Web site
rth buying just for the integrated financial tools.
financial statements or bookkeeping, the new
eat job. Not only does it give you the spreadsheets
me and expenses but it also automatically creates
hen you can take this to your CPA or accountant

had no choice but to give the seller's financial
an accountant to get the financial projections
completed. These can cost $10,000 or more.
ourself a lot of money by formatting a spread-
ating the various costs and revenues you expect
fore handing it off to the accountant.

ncial statements is nonexistent, you might feel
not worry. If you are patient and willing to read
a tool like Business Plan Pro, you will eventually
pleted.
of the tool is the ratio analysis. It analyzes your
able that illustrates the various financial ratios.
nks and investors will use to judge the viability
do is input your income and expense projec-
Business Plan Pro assembles the financial state-

atement) projections

ctions

dify certain financial projections and then use
ine the impact of the changes on the viability
ou to make the necessary changes to improve
ing financing.
ncial statements and take them to your accoun-
work. This will save you at least a thousand

dollars, perhaps more, off the bill from your accountant, because the statements from Business Plan Pro provide him or her with all the information necessary to provide you with feedback, advice, and suggestions.

The Art of Financing Your Business

The two most popular methods of financing the purchase of a business are owner financing and loans, which I discuss more below.

TIP

Other financing options include using your IRA or 401(k) proceeds to finance a business. Basically you would set up a private pension plan with the purpose of having the pension plan invest in the business. The pension plan takes ownership of the stock certificates, and you work in the business as manager.

Owner-Seller Financing

Sellers are often willing to finance a purchase of their business because they get the extra return on investment from the interest you would normally pay the bank. Plus it gives them more flexibility to sell the business to buyers the banks might not normally be willing to finance. After all who knows the business best?

My experience shows that business owners know their business potential and what it is capable of producing. Plus business owners are much more willing to take a risk than a bank. For the bank it is all about numbers; look further on in this chapter for more information on working with your banker.

If all or part of the purchase is deferred or contingent, you should expect that the seller will want to conduct some form of due diligence to investigate your business reputation, financial strength, credit history, and plans for the business.

Be conservative in the commitments you make to pay back the seller. No one can predict external events. The 2001 attack on the World Trade Center in New York had an economic impact worldwide. The United States fell quickly into a recession for a few short, but seemingly long, months. People stopped spending, trips were cancelled, and plans were put on hold. Many companies instituted a spending freeze. The trickle-down effect was enormous. You cannot plan for catastrophes, but you can get something included in your agreement so that you have some options to reduce or stop payments during tough times.

TIP

Sellers want to finance the purchase of their business because it gives them more control over how they structure the deal to take advantage of tax planning and saving a bundle of cash. When negotiating owner financing, be careful that you do not overpay for the privilege.

Be cautious in your revenue assumptions and projections. There is no guarantee that the earning potential experienced by the previous owner will continue after he leaves. That is why many former business owners provide a consulting contract for a year or two to the new owner to help ease the transition. Keeping the former owner around helps ease the shock of the business changing hands so that it is not quite so severe and customers will feel reassured, which will give you time to build your own relationship with them and keep their business intact.

TRAP

Be careful that not all the profits are being sucked out of the business to pay off debt, whether it is to the previous business owner or the bank. If your debt is too high, you have little room for error and you will not be able to cope with unforeseen circumstances as well. You need reserves to carry you through the lean times, and those reserves come from profits.

If owner financing is too expensive, you might have to walk away from the deal. The exception to this would be to build in a clause in the financing agreement that ties payments to the earnings of the company. Another approach would be to build in a clause that ties payments to certain events like economic recessions or a major accident or disaster at the business site. That way you have the option to make reduced payments. The idea is to make sure that you have enough flexibility in managing your cash flow to keep the doors open until things turn around.

Loans

If you cannot get seller financing, you will have to turn to a commercial lending institution. If this is the route you take, keep in mind that you are going to be in business for a long time and will have a relationship with a commercial loan officer throughout the life of your business. The bank is your friend. Too often I have witnessed entrepreneurs treating a lender like an adversary—like the lender does not want to loan them the money they need. Actually, it is quite the opposite: the lender wants to provide the loan. I have even heard some business owners refer to their lender as "that nosy loan officer" when all the loan officer is trying to do is understand:

- Your ability to manage and run the business
- How you intend to use the funds
- How you plan to repay the loan

Communication Is Key—Tell Your Story

If you take time to learn how commercial lending works and try to look at things from the lenders' perspective, it will help you communicate with them more effectively and make the process much more productive.

Your job is to communicate your business story to your loan officer. That is exactly what a business plan will help you do—tell your story. It is the loan officer's job to try to understand your business. You can help yourself tremendously by preparing a business plan.

TIP

This is another reason that having a business plan is important. Bring your business plan when applying for a loan: not only will it help you to tell your story to the loan officer, but you will feel much more organized, focused, and knowledgeable.

Vital Business Relationship

Just like any other important business relationship, you need to cultivate and build a quality relationship with your loan officer. Remember, these are people just like you and me. By recommending your loan they are putting their reputations and judgment on the line for you.

You are selling the ability of your business to meet its obligations and repay the loan. Be prepared to invest some time understanding how your lending institution works, the decision-making process, and how your loan officer does business. Anything you can do to build rapport and trust, and give an understanding of your business, will help your loan officer advocate your loan. On more than a few occasions I have seen the difference that a loan officer can make. If the person really wants to help you, he or she can swing the decision of a loan committee in your favor.

They Are Eager to Lend Money

A loan from a financial institution will be at much better terms than other funding alternatives such as exchanging equity (shares in your company) for investment capital or seller financing.

Assessment of Risk

A bank approaches a business loan just like every business owner does: it wants to make a profit. Unpaid loans are very expensive to a lender—for every bad loan they need 50 good loans of similar size just to breakeven.

The credit risk (probability that someone will not repay the loan) is an important part of the loan officer's job. From the lender's perspective, the true test of the creditworthiness of a borrower is his or her continued ability to repay the loan. No banker is going to be comfortable with a loan that just sits there and never gets reduced.

If your business is healthy, the probability of your not being able to repay the loan is low. However, if your credit is less than perfect, expect that this subject will dominate the discussion you have with your loan officer. The lenders' primary objective is to increase the odds that they will get back all their money *plus* a profit.

Ultimately, it is your loan officer's opinion as to what he or she thinks is going to happen that determines the interest rate, the amount of money that you can borrow, and other collateral or loan terms.

Loan Officers, Loan Committees, and You

Improving the odds of getting a business loan at the terms you want starts with understanding how a business loan is processed and approved. Understanding your role and that of your loan officer and loan committee will help you through the approval process. It is a team game, and as they say, "There is no *I* in *team*."

After your application has been submitted, your loan officer begins building a business case for your loan request. It will contain information about your business and financial condition. It will also contain information about:

- Ownership of your business
- Banking activity
- Previous borrowing experience
- Information from third-party credit reporting agencies

The document may also contain anecdotal information from your customers, competitors, or suppliers, if they happen to have a relationship with the same commercial finance organization.

Past Performance

Past financial performance, including loan repayment history, is very predictive of future financial performance. Before approving your loan request, the loan officer's job is to document this information in what is referred to as the *due diligence process* (see Chapter 20 for a details on due diligence). The loan officer will then calculate the critical financial performance ratios for the time period of your financing or business plan. Then he or she compares your ratios to that of similar companies in your industry.

Unseen Decision Makers

Most loan decisions are made by people who remain unseen by the borrower. Commercial loan officers are provided with authority to approve loans up to a certain level. Some can approve loans of $50,000 or $100,000; however, most loans over $250,000 are normally approved by a committee. Some loans over $1 million may require the approval of the board of directors.

The Loan Committee

Loan committees can have a wide range of authority. Most have little or no authority for granting loans; however, the function of those committees is to weed out loan requests before they are seen by senior management. Others have loan committees that have authority to grant loans up to the legal limit of the bank.

Most lending institutions have a relatively formal committee and decision-making process for commercial loans. Depending on the type of financial institution, your loan may be required to be submitted to a loan committee for approval.

Other banks and lending organizations provide a fairly wide scope of authority for loan officers to approve or disapprove most of the loans they handle. However, in those types of institutions the committees review the loans after they've been made. Depending on the size of the bank and its structure, the annual report may tell which directors serve on which loan committees. You may also ask your loan officer for the names and identities of the loan committee members who will be processing your loan request.

The Loan Officer's Role

Your loan officer knows you and your business the best. He or she will also have a good feel for:

- What type of loan may or may not be approved
- Types of loans
- Terms under which loans can be granted

Some loan officers are more like advocates who aggressively package, defend, and represent your loan request to the committee. Pay attention to any feedback and suggestions your loan officer provides regarding structure, information, collateral, and guarantees that will be required. Remember, your loan officer knows the rules and the organization's policies and procedures.

Plan Ahead

Do not make a last-minute request for financing. Waiting until the last minute to prepare a business plan or request for financing can hurt your chances for approval, especially if you do not have all the right information needed to make a decision.

TIP

Allow the bank or lending institution plenty of time to go through its own procedures. There is paper work, analysis of your financial statements, credit checks, etc.

It is important to have good financial management and control of your business. One of the ways you can show this is by taking the time to make a proper presentation. It is common to present your loan request with the acquisition plan (discussed in Chapter 12) detailing your vision, situation, and finance needs.

Work with the System

Many entrepreneurs and businesspeople have the perception that banks and commercial lenders do not like to lend money. Nothing could be further from the truth. They are in business to make loans—profitable loans.

Do not fight the lenders; think of them as partners. Talk to your loan officer to learn as much as you can about the approval process. Talk to other entrepreneurs and business owners who may have dealt with the organization previously. They may have insights about how the organization works and functions.

Think of your relationship with the lending institution in terms of information:

> The commercial lending institution is really an information gathering system. You have to provide assurance to the bank or lending institution that you have the capacity to repay the loan as planned.

> In your role of borrower you are the information provider. Provide them with quality information. It will help them make a decision about your loan request and help you get the money you want, at the terms you want.

Eliminate the tug-of-war and work closely with your loan officer; you will be pleased with the results.

Qualifying for a Line of Credit

A line of credit is a flexible tool that provides access to money when your company needs it. A line of credit is a flexible lending instrument secured by assets. As an example, you are approved for a ceiling of say $100,000. It allows you to run up a $100,000 "overdraft" in your operating or corporate checking account. Then when you make your bank deposit, the line of credit is repaid.

This provides a great deal of flexibility and can be a valuable buffer to pay your accounts payable before your receivables come in.

TIP

Most often, a line of credit is granted based upon sales volume and your accounts receivable (AR). Each month you report your sales and AR (there may be other reporting required as well). Based upon the amount of sales and AR, the bank calculates a percentage of your AR to determine your line of credit.

Typically, you will be lent somewhere between 20 to 30 percent of your total AR. The older your AR, the less the bank will lend. For example, amounts over 60 days will not likely be included in the calculation.

A line of credit can be secured with other assets as well, but using your AR is the most common. You will also likely be required to sign a personal guarantee. This would allow the bank to liquidate personal assets if your business failed, and the line of credit is not repaid. A personal guarantee should state the amount of the line of credit, but these days they often ask you to sign an unlimited personal guarantee. You will likely also be required to sign a letter that restricts your borrowing money elsewhere without approval.

Security and Qualifying for a Line of Credit

A line of credit can be provided either unsecured or with assets. With a secured credit line you sign a personal guarantee and pledge an asset as collateral for the loan.

For those with perfect credit an unsecured line of credit may be available. The interest rate on the loan can be a fixed rate or a variable rate that floats with the market. If secured, it will most likely be with accounts receivable, inventory, property, equipment, or fixtures. To qualify you will need to have:

- Collateral
- Established sales/earnings ratios
- Reliable and predictable cash flow

The advantage of having a line of credit is you do not have to surrender equity in your company, and the interest cost is predictable. One of its most powerful features is its flexibility. You can borrow and repay funds as your need dictates.

If you do not have collateral, a line of credit may be hard to acquire. It can also impede your ability to borrow additional funds. Because without good credit or collateral most lines of credit include restrictive covenants that limit your ability to borrow or enter into a lease contract with anyone else or at least without the bank's approval. They may require that you notify them of any significant changes in your financial position.

Using a Line of Credit

Good financial health is a great tool to have as another bank will lend you the money if your bank decides not to.

TRAP

I have clients who have obtained lines of credit at several banks in case the line of credit falls through with their current bank. Be cautious with this strategy. Having many lines of credit can be misleading. If your banker thinks your financial situation has changed significantly and checks the credit bureaus, he may be concerned to see many applications for credit elsewhere. This can hurt your credit rating.

Just remember, the bank has the right to unilaterally change the terms or cancel the line of credit at any time.

Where Should You Go for a Loan?

What is more important—small bank, large bank, or the right loan officer? The answer to this question depends on a few factors:

Small and Friendly Some banks and commercial lending institutions are more open and friendly to business credit. In some small organizations only one person deals with all commercial lending. In this case you want to carefully choose the bank and officer who deals with processing your business loan application. If you are presenting a business plan, make sure the loan officer has a business background or has the experience to understand and interpret your business plan. Otherwise they will need to call in someone else or submit it to a committee to interpret your plan.

Larger Commercial Lending Institutions These organizations typically have a number of different officers to process business credit applications. In this case you will have more options to screen who you want to do business with. Ask business people you know what bank they prefer.

Specialists There are a variety of commercial lending organizations that specialize in specific types of business financing. Some are supported and approved to make loans that are backed by a government guarantee. These government programs or guarantees are designed to help businesses that are difficult to finance or have been turned down for loans.

Ask Questions, Listen, and Learn

If you have never borrowed money for your business, be prepared to listen and learn. I highly recommend seeking out a referral from a trusted third party who can make a recommendation based on a personal experience.

Emotional Traps
Excitement

We buy things for several reasons, but every major purchase is an emotional decision. Whether we are buying a new car, home, or business, emotions have a huge influence on our decisions.

You could end up pursuing a deal further than you should at a time when you need to be more detached and analytical. Do not be afraid of taking a critical view of the business. Every time you feel an emotional tug, come back to this book and look for information to help justify the purchase in a practical way.

TRAP

If the deal is heavily weighted on the seller's side, you need a dose of reality. Stop and ask yourself whether this business opportunity, and the way it is structured, is in your best interest.

Aversion to Planning

If you have an aversion to planning, you may have a tendency to barge ahead and get things done, shoot from hip and try to figure things out as you go. Perhaps you have never seen the benefits of planning or do not know where to start. What if we change the word from planning to research? Does that make it more palatable?

There is more research involved in buying a business than there is planning. Planning happens after you have made a decision to buy the business, decided how much you are prepared to pay, figured out how you are going to make the transition, and decided what role the existing business owner will have after you take the busines over.

Know Your Limits

If you are overcommitted early in the process either financially or timewise, you could find yourself overwhelmed with the sheer amount of work and responsibilities.

TIP

Identify the gaps in skill, knowledge, and resources it will take to make the business perform to your expectations. Identify where you need to be at a certain point in time as far as employees, professional support, and systems.

Compromising to Make a Deal

It is easy to get caught up in the deal and end up making compromises that you should never have made. Be especially careful that you do not get pressured into compromising on things that are contrary to your values. For example, you could end up taking on too much liability, i.e., in a stock purchase.

Another example is when the business gets sued over an issue that happened while someone else owned the business. People do not care that you were not the owner at the time. They are suing the business, and you just happen to be the person who owns it now. This relates directly to the level of risk. Let us say that you have a business that you really like but there have been a lot of changes in the industry; i.e., the price is now too high or the market has changed a lot. Think it through. Make sure you are ready to take on that level of commitment and that this is the best time to buy.

The Right Reasons

Create balance through a number of factors. Obviously, if you cannot get the owner to agree to your terms, you will never be able to purchase the business. It is a matter of getting the right factors in place.

- Right financing.
- Right opportunity.
- Right corporate structure.
- Strike a balance between the price you pay and the potential for profit.
- Market opportunities, expanding the market the previous owner did not pursue because the owner was too busy, too tired, or just not interested.
- Examine why you want to purchase a specific business and your personal motives. Make sure that you are not emotionally trapped to buy the business and that you use logic and good analysis. Beware of indulging in self-justification.

- Once you buy the business, you are going to have it for a long time. You do not want to assume a heavy debt that leaves little room for errors.

- Get the right financing package and have a good relationship with a banker so that you can negotiate good terms. Have good financial reserves and net worth so that you can personally weather the storms that can come.

14

Does Your Business Plan Pass the Acid Test?

Market Size and Market Share

Determining the size of your market and how much market share (percentage of the market that buys from you) you need to be profitable is a crucial measurement. It can make the difference between affluence and bankruptcy.

In doing research for a client once, I discovered that the size of their market was much smaller than anticipated. When I calculated how much market share they needed to succeed, it turned out that they would have to achieve a market share of 150 percent. Everyone would have to buy their service 1.5 times! Not realistic and not achievable, so we refocused by adding markets they had not previously targeted.

The size of your market and the share of that market you can expect to sell to can be difficult to quantify. It is also very important. Let's say that your financial projections show that in order to be profitable you need to gain a 20 percent market share from current levels of 15 percent.

Gaining an additional 5 percent market does not seem like much, but if the business you are looking at buying is in a mature industry, in reality it would mean an increase of more than 33 percent. Further, mature industries are typically saturated, and gaining new market share would require taking it away from your competitors. This would likely be unrealistic and unattainable and just would not make economic sense. So what can you do in a case like this?

Reduce Expenses

If you reduce your expenses and change your plans so that you would only require a market share increase of just one-half of 1 percent (0.5 percent) you have a much more attainable and realistic goal.

Adjust Your Market Area

No business can sell to the whole world. Even an online business is only going to sell their products and services to people within a specific and definable market area. Customers in the closest proximity are going to be the most cost-effective to service. You will also be able to better penetrate the markets that are closest to you.

TIP

Sometimes you may have to expand your market area or move to a market area that better mirrors the services and products the business would offer. For example, buying a business located downtown and moving it to a suburban area with a higher concentration of your target market could be a very important strategic move. Another option would be to look into buying a business that is already located in the suburban area.

External factors

Speak to business owners and the local chamber of commerce to get a sense of the community. Try to identify specific factors, trends, or issues that may impact the business. For example, if the business is located on a highway with high visibility and traffic patterns, check the local news and civic councils to see if there are any changes anticipated to the highway route. If there are plans to change the route in a few years and you did not anticipate or plan ahead for a move, the impact could be devastating. Study the area and talk to longtime residents and business owners to see what the climate and mood is like. You might be able to pick up on an opportunity or prevent a future business crisis.

Study Sales Cycles

Every business endures sales fluctuations. By looking at the financial statements you should be able to get a sense of the sales cycles. What are the times of year that things tend to get quiet? Create a chart that shows the estimated peaks and valleys in your sales cycle. Create a plan to offset expected downturns. Try adding new products or services that allow you to tap into new markets and new revenue.

Survey and research results: you should have gained some insight from the work you did in these two areas. If your survey was well-designed and asked about buying patterns, preferences, and volumes, you should have some sort of an indicator of sales potential.

Finding Market Size the Easy Way

For a small fee ($69 in 2005) www.bizminer.com will provide you with a financial analysis profile that includes segment size and typical income statement, industry segment typical balance sheet, financial ratios (solvency, average financial ratios) profitability, efficiency, and average turnover rates. You can easily extract the information you need from this report to determine market size and market share for the business you are buying. It really is a great report and will save you a lot of time and frustration.

Estimating Market Size—Doing It Yourself

If you do not want to spend $69 for a report, you might be able to establish the size of your market through one or a combination of the many local, regional, and federal government offices that offer public access to this information. In the United States, you can access detailed financial information by industry at www.census.gov/csd/susb/susb.htm. In Canada you can try Industry Canada (http://sme.ic.gc.ca/) in conjunction with Revenue Canada they compile an "Industry Balance Sheet." Both of these sources will show you income and expense averages, gross profit, assets, and accounting ratios. Many civic governments and economic development departments also have a lot of data available that may assist you.

TIP

Many trade and industry associations monitor market size. They may sponsor or have access to industry data that will give you the size of the market.

Relevant Market Size

You cannot just state that you are participating in a market that is a $10 trillion industry nationwide. Chances are you are not buying a business with national reach. Therefore, your market reach will be limited by geography, number of competitors, and market factors. Make sure that the numbers you use are relevant to your business and industry. As long as you can explain your assumptions and they make sense, you should be safe.

If you are unable to nail down exact data, you might be able to compare your business or industry to a different industry where financial performance data is easier to obtain.

Sensitivity Analysis

One of the best ways to get a reality check is to get your CPA or accountant to prepare a cash-flow sensitivity analysis. The sensitivity analysis will reveal how sensitive and vulnerable your business is to:

- Increases in costs
- Sales slump
- Increases in revenue

Taking the time to have your accountant run a few scenarios should not cost a lot more if the accountant has prepared your cash-flow projections.

Most important—a sensitivity analysis will show you exactly how much money you will lose if sales drop by 10 percent and your costs increase by 10 percent. After all, don't you want to know this information sooner rather than later?

Cash-Flow Projections

If you are going to a bank or investor for financing, I highly recommend that you get your accountant or CPA to prepare the projected financial statements. These projections take into account the collection period for your accounts receivable (outstanding customer accounts) as well as the payment terms from your suppliers. For example, you may buy your inventory and have to pay your bills in 30 days. But you might have to wait 45 to 60 days to get paid from your customers.

A cash-flow projection will show you how much working capital you will need during those gaps in your cash position.

If you are really knowledgeable at using Microsoft Excel or another spreadsheet program, you can build your own cash-flow projections. Resist the urge to do this unless you are very analytical and very good with spreadsheets. Just one mistake can render them useless. All it takes is one number or calculation to be off, and you will not have an accurate projection of the financial position and risk.

Again, it is well worth the money to get professional help with this task from a CPA or accountant. In one case, my client's accountant accompanied him to the bank to explain the financial projections and answer any questions. The client got his loan. I am convinced the accountant's involvement was instrumental in winning the bank over.

Make the bank and accountant your friend. They are your allies and can benefit you greatly.

The Difference between Cash Flow and Profitability

Do not confuse profitability with a negative cash flow. There is a significant difference between cash flow and profit.

You can be profitable and yet have a negative cash position. It is very common for a new business to be in a negative cash-flow position for a limited period of time.

Remember, cash flow is the change in your cash balance over a specific period of time. This happens due to the difference between the amount you have to pay out and how much cash you have on hand.

Anything you buy on credit in your first month is usually payable net 30 days. Which means even though you are profitable (income – expenses = profit), your bills still have to be paid. For example, when starting a business you will most likely spend more money setting up the business than you would in a typical month, because you have to purchase inventory, raw materials, annual insurance premiums and make other expenditures that require you either purchase in bulk or prepay.

Dealing with Negative Cash-Flow Projections

The negative cash-flow projections simply indicate in advance how much money you will need to pay your bills on time. From a practical perspective your options are:

1. Arrange in advance with your bank to grant you a line of credit to cover the shortfall.

2. Negotiate deferred or longer payment terms with your suppliers for your start-up expenses.

If you expect a lot of employee turnover, a common strategy is to withhold your employees' first one or two week's pay. In other words, they are always one or two weeks in arrears. Note: I advise that you place this amount in a payroll reserve account which would be paid to the employees when they quit or are laid off. Also, check with your local labor regulations to make sure you can do this.

I would also suggest that you look at the rest of the year. Is your cash-flow position improving? Is there a point when your cash flow is positive? If your cash flow keeps getting larger, you either have some expenses duplicated or errors in your entries. You need to show when the cash flow situation will improve, be able to justify your situation, and explain it to the satisfaction of your banker or investor. Take the time to review your entries item by item. Make sure that you have confidence in the cash-flow projections. Keep adjusting your expenses until it makes sense to you.

PART 5

BUYING A BUSINESS STEP-BY-STEP

15

Approaching Business Owners

Who Are You?
Why Should I Care?

Make Sure You Are Organized

New tasks will arise continually. Throughout all the interactions and information you are exposed to, you will find that one new piece of information will likely lead you to another question that must be answered. If you do not write these down and assign the follow-up, it simply will not get done.

Remember, you do not have to do this alone. You will need the help of your accountant. Plus I recommend that you not get bogged down with the "grunt" work. Tasks like counting inventory or chasing down information is something that can be completed by someone else. You should look at hiring a friend or family member to help you with these tasks. You may think that a small business would be easy to keep organized, but you will be surprised at how disorganized some businesses actually are.

Before You Approach the Owner

Sooner or later you will need to approach a business owner about buying his or her business.

On the basis of your research and an industry analysis, you have identified a business you want to learn more about. How do you approach the business owner?

The business owner may or may not have been thinking about selling the business. On the other hand, if you found the business for sale through a newspaper ad or another advertisement, your approach is much simpler. Regardless, you want to make a good impression and get things off to a good start. What are you going to say or do?

State Your Purpose and Be Accommodating

Put yourself in the seller's position. You get a phone call from someone asking to meet with you to discuss selling the business.

First, your phone call is an interruption so this may not be the best time for them. Owners may be in their office, or they could be in the middle of an important task. Second, they are probably thinking something along these lines: "Who are you and why should I care?" Being very flexible and accommodating in the beginning will go a long way to building trust and rapport with a seller.

Some personalities, especially analytical types, may procrastinate in setting up a meeting. They might seem like they are avoiding you when in reality they are thinking about how they should handle your inquiry and about a number of other issues. You can bet that they will be asking themselves if they are ready to sell and if so, how much the business is worth.

TIP

Do not try to manipulate the seller into setting up a meeting or come across as demanding. Tell them you realize your call has likely caught them off guard. State that you are only asking for an initial meeting so that you can get to know one another, and that you are not expecting a commitment from them at that meeting. Tell them you are just asking for a meeting to see if there is some common ground to pursue this further.

The First Meeting

Allow the seller to control the agenda, for now.

Early on, your role is all about selling yourself. Share information about your background, skills, and experience, but before you start telling the seller everything you think they need to know about you—slow down. Let the seller lead.

Most likely the seller will get right into asking you questions. You should be prepared to answer questions and inquiries: Here's what you might expect.

- The seller might ask "What interested you about buying my business?" Keep your answers general but not so vague that you are avoiding giving them a straight answer. Tell them what you have learned about the business in the community. Also, tell them your personal reasons for wanting to buy a business.

- The seller will also want to know more about you, your experience and plans. Answer these questions as directly as you can without revealing any of your strategic plans. For example, you can talk about your previous experience and background. Then close your answer stating something like "It is too early to know how things might go, but I think we should continue our discussions to explore this opportunity further. Don't you agree?"

- Sellers will be curious about the price you are willing to pay, or they may tell you how much they would need in order to sell the business. Be clear with them about your goals and expectations. Again, let the seller take the lead.

TIP

The truth is that sellers have more control in the beginning because they have the leverage of saying or pretending that they are not interested. But if they were not interested then why would they agree to meet? The truth is they are curious and are just being cautious.

Practice Professional Detachment

Maintain your perspective and professional detachment. I keep repeating the professional detachment refrain, because without it you can easily lose perspective. Without perspective, your ability to make tough decisions drops exponentially.

TRAP

Avoid allowing yourself to get excited prematurely. It will cloud your judgment. A business deal can go sideways for any number of reasons.

Learn to balance your excitement and passion for the business with old-fashioned self-control. Emotion skews perspective. If you start justifying your excitement, it may already be too late to regain your independent perspective. You better make darn sure you maintain that ability or surround yourself with advisers and friends who will argue with you if they feel you have lost perspective.

TIP

It is easy to pay too much for a business. The strongest negotiating strategy is being prepared to walk away from any deal. There is incredible freedom in saying no.

Remember, as the buyer, you do not have to do or agree to anything unless it is in your best interest. If it is not in your interest, why compromise?

At the end of the day there is nothing quite so painful as knowing that you made a bad decision and had the opportunity to say no and didn't. If you choose to compromise just to make a deal and it does not work out, you will be the only person to blame because you made the commitment and allowed yourself to be sold.

TRAP

The danger of being sold happens innocently. It begins when a personal dream seems to align magically with what appears to be a wonderful opportunity. Be cautious because if you lose perspective, you can end up doing almost anything to get what you want.

Every business is for sale for a reason. It is easy to buy a business in trouble, but significantly more difficult to buy a healthy business. If the deal seems too good to be true, what have you overlooked? What do you not know? Think about it, why would someone want to sell a profitable business? If there is a good reason, you have to find out what the reason is.

Sometimes it's as simple as a change in priorities. After working most of their lives, business owners find themselves looking at their sunset years and wanting a change. Maybe they simply want more freedom to pursue a hobby or special interest. Health concerns can change priorities instantly. All things being equal there must be a good reason to sell a business.

Matchmaking Made Easy

Playing the matchmaking game is serious business. Business deals go sideways every day. The seller may disagree with your plans for the business, or you or the seller may feel insulted and decide to back out. Perhaps you uncover a debt or liability that could expose you to unacceptable financial risk.

For example, a business operating without workers' compensation insurance is exposed to serious liabilities. If sued, a loss case could put you out of business. What if there was a serious onsite accident that caused injury to an employee? Maybe the employee has not yet sued for medical bills or negligence, but the person could. If you buy the business and the person does decide to sue, he or she will sue the business and current owner. Guess what? That's you.

Negotiate Using Open-Ended Questions

When buying a business, the right information is the lubricant that keeps things rolling because it can help you make informed decisions and anticipate potential problems. It is the answer to a well-formed and well-timed question that makes for a powerful negotiator. Why? Because answering an open-ended question requires an explanation and this can provide insights about the seller and the business that can be used to your advantage.

An open-ended question cannot be answered with a yes or no because more detail is required. Further, it would be rude to answer an open-ended question with a yes or no. This simple strategy will help you gain the advantage while providing you with the information you need.

The Right Question Reveals Everything

Open-ended questions begin with words such as "why" and "how" or phrases such as "What do you think about . . .?" Open-ended questions should lead the listener to answer with detail and make the person think.

One of the things I find most fascinating about businesspeople is that they do not expect you to know everything. If you have the ability to ask good questions, respect for you grows.

TIP

I have found that by posing well-formed, open-ended questions business owners will teach me everything I need to know about the business and their situation. Through these questions we both learn something, and most important, trust is built. Right or wrong, business owners assume that if you can ask good questions, you must have considerable knowledge.

I have found there is nothing more powerful than a focused, well-formed, open-ended question. It still amazes me after all these years. Best of all, if you have rapport, you will be pleasantly surprised at what the owner is willing to tell you. You can learn anything from anyone if you ask the right question. Have fun!

Forming Open-Ended Questions

Think about what you want to know. Then form questions using "why" and "how" or phrases such as "What do you think about . . .?" The number and types of questions you can ask using this strategy are endless. If you do not understand the answer they give to your question, ask them to clarify: "I do not understand . . ." or "Could you expand on that?"

Other options include "Tell me about your . . .," "What else can you do . . .?" "What could you use to . . .? What do you think would happen if . . .? Is there another way to . . .?" Just add an ending to your question relating to the issue you would like to learn more about.

Open-ended questions are probing in nature, and it is a good idea to take time to get to know one another with simple questions first, especially if this is the first time you have met. Each person is nervous and the less threatening your questions, the faster you will be able to build rapport (trust). You can read more about open-ended questions in Chapter 17.

When you feel ready to begin asking your open-ended questions I suggest that you preframe the topic by making a statement that seeks their permission. Something like, "As you can imagine I have a lot of questions. If it is all right with you I would like to get started. Please let me know if you feel uncomfortable answering any question. Feel free to ask me why I might be asking that question." Remember, if they feel uncomfortable answering your questions, you will not get the answers you need and worst of all, they might be offended.

TIP

You need to be conscious of body language and demeanor. If you notice the business owner fidgeting, looking at his or her watch, getting quiet for a long period, or quickly changing facial expression, just let it go. Simply state something like, "I hope my question was not too presumptuous." This should take the pressure off and they just might answer the question. They might simply be feeling that they need to get back to work or you may have touched on a sensitive topic.

If you really need an answer to the question try to revisit it at some other time. If they simply refuse to answer either you have lost rapport (your first task is to regain trust) or there is something they do not wish to reveal to you at this time. If you perceive it is the latter, you should ask yourself what this tells you about the situation and what it might mean to your plans for continuing to pursue this venture.

Getting the Seller's Attention

One of the most powerful tools to get peoples' attention is to understand how they like to be approached. Business owners, like everyone else, are naturally resistant to change. By understanding their preferences for dealing with change, you will set a natural foundation of trust.

Everyone has a natural preference for dealing with change. When confronted with change, we search our frame of reference to make comparisons in an effort to grasp how this change might impact our lives.

Basically, people judge how change may impact them in accordance with their preferences for "sameness" or "difference."

Sameness People

Sameness people look for something in their lives they perceive as being the "same" as their current situation. It comforts them and gives them a frame of reference to decide how they want to proceed. In the conversation listen for a comment they make that you could use to illustrate how a certain idea is similar to something in their lives.

For example, if you asked them "How did you make the transition from a one-man operation to the business you have now?" they might answer by telling you how they purchased their building and what the important decisions were along the way. I would then rephrase what they said and state, "I guess selling your business is the same as when you purchased your building. You had to put a lot of time and energy into the project before you knew how it would turn out. Isn't that like our situation? We each have to do a certain amount of work to figure out what our next steps should be." How they respond to that statement will give you a good sense of how things are going so far. Plus, your statement refers back to something they said, which is flattering. Everyone wants to feel important, including business owners. They have egos too.

For every rule there are exceptions. In the group of people who tend toward seeing how things are the same, there is also a subset who will notice similarities first and then see how things are different. In this case you can use analogies that demonstrate how what you want to do is the same as one of the experiences they shared with you. Then point out the differences.

Be careful not to peg people as being a sameness or differences type and then forget to watch for a change. People do grow and change, sometimes right before your eyes.

Differences People

Differences people see how things are "different." You may not meet many of these people, as they are the minority. Differences people are very successful and make good businesspeople. I think Thomas Edison saw how things were different. After all, who else would state—after trying over 1000 different filaments before he found one that would work—that "I now know 1000 different ways how not to build a light bulb."

You can pick differences people out in a conversation because they seem to contradict themselves and the opinions expressed by others during a conversation. They are not as flaky as they might appear. It is just that their first reaction to taking in information is to look into their life experience and how what is going on is different. They pride themselves on their ability to adapt, and they are good at it. They are intuitive and creative. Communicating with them can be confusing and challenging because they will, quite literally, mismatch most of the population.

Differences people love change and want more of it. These people are constantly reorganizing; if they do not get enough change, they will quit and go somewhere else. They will change something for the sake of change.

Tell them how you see what they have done with the business is different and that there is an opportunity still to do something new and radically different. They like uniqueness and difference. Using scarcity can influence them greatly.

In the group of difference people is a subset that will first notice how things are different and then see the similarities. Like the main group they enjoy change and variety. They can see both how things are the same and yet different at the same time. Tell them the way you manage and run the company is going to be different but how, on many levels, it will be the same; how it combines the best of both worlds. You could speak to how you will need to make changes based upon your plans but that you share the same values when it comes to hiring and managing employees. This provides them with a bit of information about your plans and proposed changes, while illustrating that you also share common beliefs.

Listen and Then Try a Strategy

As strange as the idea of preferring sameness or difference may seem to you, figuring out which personality type your prospect is really does help smooth out the gaps in human communication.

Observe the types of words your prospect is using. They will give you clues to whether they are sameness or difference people. Then try one of the above strategies until you find one that seems to connect with them.

16
Understanding the Seller's Situation

The Seller as the Biggest Obstacle

The reason so many business owners continue to operate a business long after they can afford to retire is the great satisfaction and sense of purpose they get from managing their business. They love the business and for many it is the most meaningful part of their lives outside their families. Selling the business means they will lose that connection. Further, just considering selling the business forces them to consider the future. If they have not taken the time to think through what it means to be retired, this could cause negotiations to come to a complete stop for a period of time.

If you found the business for sale through advertising, you will know the price and likely the reason the business is for sale. The seller has already made a decision to sell and is prepared to meet with prospective buyers. For the most part, you can meet with the owner and ask a few questions to get the information you need to decide whether or not you want to pursue it further.

If you have been using this book, you have likely located a business for sale through some research or a referral from someone you know. The owner may or may not be ready to sell the business. They may not even be ready to seriously consider the possibility. However, they may be curious about why you want to buy the business and how much you think it is worth, and for right now that is enough. But, if things are going to proceed further, then the seller has a lot of things to consider, including still running the business. If he or she cannot get past that point you will go nowhere in your discussions.

Move Negotiations Along by Helping the Seller

I know all you want to do is get on with buying the business. But the impact of the change in ownership will dominate the sellers' thinking until they resolve it in their own minds. At this point sellers are interested enough that they are willing to meet with you. They are wondering why you want to buy the business and how much you think it is worth.

If you were to ask sellers if they need help working this out, they would probably tell you not to worry, that they just need some time—time to think about their future plans and what it will mean to their life when the business is sold. You can help the seller along by helping them see what is possible and what it will mean for them when they do sell the business.

Why Help the Seller?

Why should you get involved in helping the seller work this out? Until they can see how selling to you is going to help them achieve their goals, you will not be able to get them to make the decision to proceed past the most basic discussions. Therefore, if you do not want your progress to slow to a crawl, you need to be prepared to help sellers voice their concerns and find answers to their questions.

Move from Necessity Thinking to Possibilities Thinking

Out of necessity, you have a specific timeline and plan to keep it, and are ready to get on with gathering the information you need to decide if you want to or can buy the business. The biggest difference between your perspective and that of a successful business owner is that they are not in a hurry.

Since you enquired if they would meet to discuss the possibility of selling their business, I guarantee the seller is thinking about their future plans and what selling the business will mean to them. They're also likely thinking about all of the things that they will be able to do with the money from the sale. While this is going on in the seller's mind, you will be thinking about how to move the process forward.

Necessity Thinking

Necessity thinking is needs-based. Something has prompted a new awareness of a specific need. In this case you make contact with the business
owner to enquire if the person would consider selling the business. Your
request has stirred an awareness of something they do not have or a need
that has not been met yet. Necessity thinking is narrowly focused on basic
needs and emotions—what is needed for survival.

Possibility Thinking

Possibility thinkers look beyond survival to what is possible, what can be
achieved. On any particular day we can be in a place where we are definitely thinking about our basic necessities. But then something happens and we
shift to possibilities.

When we are looking at a major change in our lives, we tend to remain
in either necessity or possibilities mode. Dealing with a business owner
who is in a place of possibilities is quite different than dealing with the
one who is stuck in necessity thinking. By making simple adjustments to
the words you use and how you phrase questions, you can make a substantial difference in the quality of the conversation and the owner's willingness to embrace change.

The Difference between Necessity
and Possibility Thinking

When people are in a place of necessity, they are thinking about their most
urgent or essential needs. The last thing you would do in speaking with
them is to share your vision, ideas, or excitement. That would break rapport
and create doubt because they are thinking of themselves and hearing your
ideas seems insensitive.

You will run into sellers that are stuck in a place of necessity because the
business is struggling. When communicating with them speak directly to
the need, concern, or issues at hand. For example, ask them, "If you do not
sell the business or sales do not improve, you will eventually have to close
the business. Right? On the other hand if we can come to an agreement,
you can sell the business and move on with your life with some cash."

If you were meeting with a successful business owner this statement would
clearly be inappropriate, because they will be more opportunity and possibility focused. In that case you would change your approach to something
like, "Based on our telephone discussion I can see that you are interested
but had not been thinking about selling. I see an opportunity for both of us.

You would get to enjoy the fruit of your labor and know that someone is looking after the business you built. By the way, what would you do with your time if you sold the business?" This would encourage owners to share their plans and dreams. Obviously, there is a big difference in the tone between the two conversations.

TIP

Align yourself with the seller. If they are in a possibility frame of mind, shift your questions toward probing the exciting opportunities or plans they might have after the sale. When dealing with sellers in a place of necessity adjust your language and questions to probe more about all the hard work they have done and how they got to this point. Discuss how frustrating it must be for them to be in this situation and position the sale of the business as an escape.

Understand the Psychology Driving a Business Owner

The five senses: sight, hearing, touch, smell, and taste are what we use to observe the world around us. We use five senses to perceive things and it forms the foundation for how we learn.

Our five sensory systems are referred to by the acronym VAKOG, which is short for visual, auditory, kinesthetic, olfactory and gustatory. Each person tends toward one primary strategy for processing information. For example:

- V = Visual (sight). Visual people prefer visual mediums. Typically they are meticulous in their dress and appearance. They learn best by seeing and watching other people actually do a task. They remember faces, what a person wears, but they do not necessarily remember the name of the person that goes with the face. They like to make lists, doodle, and visualize and may point a lot. You will find they use visual phrases to indicate approval including, "Looks good to me," or "That brightens up my day," and "I see what you mean."

- A = Auditory (hearing). Auditory people enjoy a good lecture, instructions, and talks with others. They learn best by listening. They have a good auditory memory, and they are typically good at remembering names, details of what was said but not the faces of the people they meet. Auditory people are easily distracted by ambient sounds. They often notice changes in voice tone and pitch in others and themselves as emotions change. You can see them tilt their head to the left or right when they are listening to something important. They take pleasure in praise, quiet surroundings, and natural sounds. They use phrases like "Sounds good to me" and "I hear you loud and clear" to indicate acceptance or agreement.

- K = Kinesthetic (feeling). Kinesthetic people learn best by remembering feelings. They tend to fidget a lot and squirm. They need room to move around and be comfortable. They like to touch, feel, manipulate, and try things out. They enjoy comfortable clothes, furniture, and physical contact. When communicating with them, you will need to draw them out by showing them something they can touch or using phrases like, "How do you feel about this?" Or you could hear them say something like "That felt great!" or "Get a grip."

- O = Olfactory (smell). You will find a lot of olfactory people working in restaurants or in wine or liquor sales. They will speak in more concrete terms and say things like "The whole deal stinks" or "Like a dog following a scent."

- G = Gustatory (taste). Gustatory people say things like "It's very tasty." When describing something they liked, they would state that they "were just drooling." Disapproval gets voiced with statements like "That left a sour taste in my mouth."

Shift Your Style to Mirror the Seller's VAKOG Preferences

Visual people tend to be big-picture people who think more in concepts and pictures. They look for visual references to explain past events or decisions. Make sure you are dressed well and well groomed. You can bet that they will be. They tend to dislike a lot of detail, and they will make quick decisions as soon as they feel they have enough information.

When meeting with a seller who you realize is visual, all you need to do is start using words that are more visual or a combination that paints a word picture.

Auditory people like to hear the sound of their own voice. They enjoy conversations with people and make decisions based upon what they hear not what they see. A noisy restaurant would not be a good place to have an important conversation with them. Because they are so focused on the auditory they tend to pick up changes in voice pitch and tone so they can easily pick up the changing emotions of others. They tend to think of themselves as being more intuitive.

For the auditory seller, listen carefully to what they are saying. When you find something they mentioned on which you have some information you can share with them, say something like "I hear you. I was reading an article the other day. . . ." Connect with them using words and phrases like "I hear you," "That sounds interesting," or something similar, and you will be amazed how well they will respond.

The kinesthetic person is a friendly, social person who takes in the world around them based upon how they feel. They tend to be quiet, sometimes withdrawn, because they are busy processing what is going on inside them.

The kinesthetic seller is the one type that is most influenced by body language. This will require spending time with them and listening to their feelings and connecting with them. Be patient, because these people are very loyal.

Olfactory and gustatory people are highly experiential and make great candidates to take to a fine restaurant for a meeting. Their experience of being with you will be heightened by the addition of pleasant tastes and smells. Because they rely so heavily on the experiential aspect of relationships, they prefer to do things with people in an effort to get to know them. They are passionate people with strong opinions. The olfactory and gustatory people will appreciate a meal in a nice restaurant or a glass of wine.

Making these subtle shifts in a conversation can help to build rapport and trust early in the process. There will be more of a connection between both parties and communication will be a lot clearer.

Keeping Notes

I have found that keeping written notes can be invaluable, especially when it comes time to create your letter of intent, which upon signing by both parties begins the formal due diligence period (see Chapter 20). Make notes of any comments made by the seller that strike you as odd. You will want to investigate them during the due diligence period.

I prefer a hard-cover notebook because the pages are sewn into the hardcover binding and cannot fall out. If I collect pieces of paper along the way, I simply tape them onto a page in the notebook. These notebooks can usually be found in your local stationery store.

TIP

I always write my name and phone number in the notebook and state that I will pay a reward to the person returning it to me.

17
Preliminary Negotiations Begin

Negotiating to buy a business is more complex than and different from any other major purchase you may have had experience with. A business succeeds because the owner found a way to tough it out during the lean times and kept refining the business until he or she found a formula that met the needs of the marketplace and was profitable. This creates a lot of emotional attachment to the business, staff, and suppliers.

This is an important factor because the emotional attachment a seller has to the business is going to impact your negotiations. I have had many owners express their concern about how the plans the buyer has for the business will affect staff and suppliers.

TRAP

Business owners know their business inside and out because it has been a part of their lives for a long time. If you have planned major changes in the business that involve staff or suppliers, make sure you have done your homework. I have seen deals die because owners were not willing to risk the jobs of their staff after the business is sold. The last thing you want is to have the owner challenge your ideas and insist on a clause to protect the employees' jobs as part of your sales agreement. It could tie your hands and be counterproductive.

Remember, when you buy a business not only do you get the keys to the kingdom you also get assets, customers, and suppliers. All of these come with a big dose of new obligations. The seller's perspective is going to be different than yours because on some level he or she has to consider the impact that the sale of the business will have on the people the owner has established relationships with over a number of years.

TIP

I have met many business owners who have told me running a business is like getting married, buying a house, and running a day care. This reflects the level of commitment and care they have toward the people who have helped them build the business. They will want to protect these people as much as possible.

Let the Seller Talk

Business owners are very protective and determined to find someone who thinks like they do. They will go to great lengths in an attempt to screen out the riffraff. Their identity is so wrapped up in the business that they will want to know your plans for their business. This is where you need to be careful to share enough to gain the seller's confidence. On the other hand, be careful that you do not share too much about your plans, especially if the areas in which you have planned to make major changes are something you know the owner is sensitive about.

TIP

If you are going to be having the seller finance the business, do not be surprised if you are asked for a written business plan detailing your goals and plans. If this is the case, you will need to be open with the seller about your plans and changes the owner can expect. Owner financing will bring a higher level of accountability and involvement of the seller during negotiations and after the sale.

Information Gathering Questions

As discussed in Chapter 15, open-ended questions will help you to get the seller talking and get the information you need to make an informed buying decision. Here are some questions you can use as a guide to form your own open-ended questions.

General Questions

- "Why did you start this business?"

- "If you had the opportunity to start the business now, what would you do differently?" Answers to this question could help you to identify problems, opportunities, and perhaps reveal their real reason for selling.

- "What do you see as the greatest challenge running the business?" This answer may help you understand the owner's strengths, weaknesses, and difficulties running this type of business.

- "How did the first few years in business go?" Quite often how the owner handled the first few years will reveal a lot about the decisions made and how the owner ended up where he or she is now. It could also give you more ideas for other questions you need answers to.

Specific Questions

- "What prompted you (your company) to look into selling at this time?" Depending on the reason for selling you may or may not get a straight answer to this question. For example, if owners are having health problems, they may not want to reveal it in case you view it as an opportunity to lowball them on the price.

- "What are your expectations or requirements from me in this process?" This question will show an openness and willingness to work with them. The exchange of information should be a two-way street, and I think you will find them more open to providing the details you need if you open up too.

- "What type of person would be the best successor to run your business?" They will have a strong emotional attachment to the business and be protective of which person they "allow" to buy the business. Remember, until they accept your formal offer, they still have the keys.

- "What would you like to accomplish over the next 90 days?" Often timelines can make or break a deal, and knowing their expectations on when they would like to know how serious your intentions are would be good to know.

- "What process did you go through to determine your selling price?" This might be a difficult question for them to answer, or it may be as simple as their saying, "That is how much I need to walk away from the business."

- "If we are successful in our negotiations, how do you see the transition happening?" They might have an expectation of staying on during the transition as a consultant. This is a good thing and would make things go smoothly. Make sure to include any consulting fees or salary that will be paid to the previous owner as part of the total price.

- "If you have had negotiations with others in the past, how did it go? Are you still actively pursuing that buyer?" If the business has been on the market for some time it may indicate an owner that is difficult to deal with or is unrealistic in his or her expectations. Understand that you may or may not get a straight answer to this question. Observe their body language. Watch their eyes: if they glance away or squirm, they might not be answering your question. This is not uncommon. It is not that they are lying but it is in their best interest not to answer the question. But you can still ask it.

- "As far as staff go, with whom have you had difficulties with in the past? Is the situation resolved?" The owner will have a perspective on the staff situation that could be helpful to you.

- "Can you please explain staff benefits, vacations, and payroll?" You will want to know the track record the owner has in dealing with staff. Benefits are a good indicator of how they treat employees.

- "How is your company organized, from a securities perspective (i.e., LLC, S-Corp etc.)?" The corporation they have now might affect your strategy, especially if you are doing a stock purchase.

- "Why did you choose that structure?" Answers to this question will range from "That is what my attorney or CPA recommended." to "A few years ago I did some tax planning and reorganization." In a case like this I would want to review changes that were made and get them evaluated by a CPA or attorney who specializes in tax planning. It could work out well for you or it may present some challenges for a stock purchase, and an asset purchase may be your best option.

- "If you had the time, what do you think could be improved in the business?" Knowing what gaps they see in the operation will tell you part of what you will need to deal with during the takeover.

- "What do you see as the most significant changes that have impacted the business since starting?" If there have been a lot of industry changes or external events that have affected the business negatively, you might want to rethink buying this business. If the current owner has not been able to overcome these issues, what makes you think you could fare any better? Not that you cannot, just make sure you have looked at this issue from all angles.

- "Can you tell me what type of structure you are planning for the sale of your business? Sale of the assets or a sale of the shares?" Then follow up with, "Why, is that choice important to you?" If they are set on a stock purchase and you are not interested in that type of deal, it would be better to know this sooner than later.

- "What are your plans after selling the business?" They may have travel plans, dreams, and perhaps they are planning to start another business. If you need them to stay on for a few years as a consultant to the business, you may need to have your attorney come up with some wording in the agreement to protect your interests.

- "Which of your employees do you consider indispensable and why?" This person could be an invaluable asset in the purchasing process as well as the transition. It would be someone you get along with and stays after the takeover.

- "If you had the opportunity to change one thing about the industry or business, what would it be and why would that be important?" This answer might reveal a core weakness or problem that this particular business copes with or it could be something that affects every business in this industry. Knowing this can help you plan ahead for it.

Questions to Clarify Answers to Open-Ended Questions

- "How does that work now?"
- "Can you help me understand that situation a little better?"
- "What does that mean?"
- "What do you view as the best thing about that?
- "What challenges has that created for you personally?"
- "What other items should we discuss?"
- "Why do you continue?"
- "Did you say . . . ?"

TIP

Pay attention to the tone of your voice, inflection, and body language. A question can come across as insensitive and rude if delivered inappropriately. The types of questions you ask and how you ask them makes an impression. The quality of your questions will reveal your agenda, create a healthy conversation, and build your credibility.

The more you prepare your questions in advance and put them in writing, the more attention you can put into listening to answers. It is appropriate to refer to written questions and also make notes. If the seller is interested in having you buy the business, the seller will not have a problem with your notes or questions.

Potential Pitfalls

Seller Financing and Debt

As discussed in Chapter 13, many small business sales are owner-financed because that gives the seller the opportunity to structure a deal using a tax-efficient strategy. However, owner-financed businesses often end up carrying more debt than other businesses, because there is no third party (i.e., banker) making sure that the business passes a basic viability test that includes paying taxes and repaying its debts.

If the owner-financed business carries too much debt, you will be forced to use the business's profits to pay the previous owner. This could tie your hands, with little financial room for error or to cope with unforeseen circumstances. Profits are what carry a business through the lean times. If the profits are used up making loan payments, you will have little flexibility during tough times and your risk of failure will increase substantially. In these cases you would be better off making a deal to purchase the assets and find your own financing or walk away from the deal altogether.

TRAP

Taking advantage of seller financing can be a great opportunity, but have a good financial plan put together by your CPA to make sure you can afford to pay back the loans. Otherwise, if the business faltered slightly due to events beyond your control, all the profits could be sucked out to pay off the loan due the previous owner.

Lack of Direct Experience

If you are purchasing a business that you have no direct experience in running, you should examine your motive. I have been guilty of this myself. I have started businesses that I knew little about and had to learn my way through. You can succeed if you are prepared to do a lot of work and take on the risk.

You will need to get the experience somehow. Baptism by fire can be an unpleasant thing and in business this type of situation will usually result in lower sales, profits, and cash flow. Moreover, the effect on you personally could be significant.

Not Enough Capital

Being underfinanced can be a real challenge because the lack of cash may prevent you from making the changes you need to be profitable. There are success stories of people who have taken risks, turned things around, and survived despite being underfunded, but think about whether you are willing to take that risk.

Be careful of what you are willing to compromise to make a deal. If you think that owning a business is an easy way to make money, just make sure that you are prepared to pay the price to get the results you need. You could be betting everything you own on a poor hand.

Compromising to Make a Deal

It is easy to get caught up in the deal and end up making compromises that you should never have considered. One example is taking on too much liability.

If you are doing a stock purchase, you are buying the stocks (shares) of the company. When you purchase these stocks, you are essentially taking over ownership and operation of that corporation and assuming the liabilities of the previous owner (except in the case of fraud or a criminal act). Let's say you were thinking of a stock purchase and in your research you discover that there had been a spill of some kind. If the cleanup was not done properly, there could be a future liability. If you know this going into the deal, you should have the current owner deal with the issue, or deduct the cost of the cleanup from the asking price.

Another example of liability is when the business gets sued over an issue that happened while someone else owned the business. People do not care that you were not the owner at the time. They are suing the business, and you just happen to be the person who owns it now. This relates directly to the level of risk.

If you do identify potential future liabilities, a good strategy is to withhold a portion of the price "in trust" for a specific period of time.

TRAP

Be especially careful if you have compromised on things that are contrary to your values. Take time to think it through. Make sure you are ready to take on that level of commitment. Is this the best time for you to be buying this business?

Balancing Risk and Rewards

Obviously, if you cannot get the owner to agree to your terms, you will never be able to purchase the business. It is a matter of getting the right factors in place.

- Right financing.

- Right opportunity.

- Workable corporate structure.

- Balance between the price you pay and the profit potential.

- Market opportunities, expanding the market the previous owner did not pursue because they were too busy, too tired, or just not interested.

- Examine why you want to purchase a specific business and your personal motives. Make sure you are not emotionally trapped to buy the business. Also be sure to use logic and good analysis.

- Have a healthy net worth so that you can personally weather the storms that can come with owning a business if you are unable to pay your salary for a period of time.

- Once you buy the business, you are going to have it for a long time. You do not want to assume a heavy debt that leaves little room for errors.

- Find a banker with whom you have a good relationship. It will help a great deal toward making sure you get the right financing package (plus you can likely negotiate better terms with a banker who likes you).

18

Overcoming Roadblocks and Obstacles and Identifying Deal Breakers

If you followed my advice at the end of Chapter 16, you should have some notes on areas of concern. Before your attorney drafts a letter of intent, go through these notes. In Chapter 19 we will discuss the letter of intent in detail.

Review and Organize Your Notes

Grab a highlighter and go through your notes page by page. Mark notes that require verification and further explanation. Once you have done a thorough review of your notes, sit down with a pen, your favorite beverage, and a fresh page of your notebook. List any new items that you have thought of as you were reviewing and marking up your notes.

Review the highlighted notes and categorize them using a numerical system. Each number represents a major area of the business. For example:

1. Operations
2. Employees
3. Customers
4. Suppliers
5. Management

6. Assets

7. Liabilities

8. Financial

9. Legal

Go through your notes and mark each item with the appropriate category number. When I do this I circle the item to make sure I do not miss it when I transfer it to a spreadsheet.

After the categorization is complete, I sit down in front of a computer to transfer items one by one to a worksheet in Excel that matches the categorization scheme I am using. I prefer a spreadsheet program to a word processing program because it can sort and categorize items into separate worksheets and toggle between them. The added benefit of a spreadsheet (Excel) is its ability to create pivot tables that sort and organize the information even further.

TIP

To find out more about using pivot tables in Excel, look in the help section of the program itself. For the more detail minded, you could also pick up a book on Excel that will show you how to use a pivot table.

A word processing program could serve a similar purpose if you categorize each note into a separate file. But you will not get the advantage of creating pivot tables.

Spreadsheet Setup

I use a landscape setup to take advantage of the extra horizontal space on a sheet of paper. I find 8.5" by 14" paper is best. From left to right I set up my spreadsheet with the following columns:

- Item Number: Numerical marking for easy referencing.
- Activity Title: Write a short but descriptive one- or two-word title of the activity item.
- Description: This is a short but more detailed description of the issue. I like to list my goal, i.e., the ideal outcome, here as well. If there is not enough room, I might set up an additional column titled Goal.
- Outcome: Here I diarize the outcome or what I learned as a result of the activity.

- Resources: I list the resources I might need. For example, doing a financial review I would list the documents to be supplied by the seller.

- People: These are individuals who I think will have the information I need so I can investigate this further.

- Documents Required: This column is where you will make a list of all the documents you need to conduct your due diligence when it starts. This list of documents required will eventually become a part of the letter of intent or offer to purchase that your attorney will create.

TRAP

If you do not think of all the documents you will need before you start the process, things will get missed. Unfortunately, this usually translates into unwanted surprises or extra costs later on. Take time to do it right the first time.

Data Entry

Now that you have your spreadsheet setup, you can sit down and transfer the numbered items from your notebook. As I transfer each one, I put an *X* through the numbered and circled item I marked earlier. This way I can review the notes when I am finished to make sure I have not missed any items.

Roadblocks, Obstacles, and Deal Breakers Defined

Roadblocks

A Roadblock makes it difficult for you to make progress or achieve your objective of buying the business. These are time wasters and annoying situations that make life difficult. Some examples are:

1. Lack of current monthly financial statements. If I have to wait for an accountant or bookkeeper to prepare the financial statements for the last year that could be a deal breaker. With the accounting programs now available there is no good reason for a company to be three months or more in arrears on its accounting. (Note: if it is just a month or two behind, it is just an annoyance and can happen to any business. A bookkeeper can be sick or leave. You just have to be patient and wait.)

2. Poor filing system. If the owner cannot locate important documents (contracts, etc.), it does raise concerns but this is not a deal breaker. The

seller can always request a copy from the supplier or manufacturer. On the other hand, if a contract with an employee is missing that could be more serious. If you cannot view the wording in the contract, you cannot ascertain the risk or associated liability.

3. Inability of the seller to answer certain questions. If I am asking questions about the business and am unable to get an answer from the seller, either he does not know the answer or hopes the question will go away. In the latter instance this may simply reveal a character flaw.

Obstacles

An obstacle is something or someone that stands in the way and must be circumvented in order to get the information I need to verify the assumptions I have made about the business or statements made by the seller. Here are some examples of obstacles:

1. Failure to get questions answered. If I am repeatedly unable to get a straight answer from the seller, either he does not know the answer or hopes the questions will go away. If I feel that he is preventing me from getting the information and answers I need, then I might escalate this issue to a deal breaker.

2. Lack of cooperation. In the due diligence process, lack of cooperation from employees and management would be a significant obstacle, which left unattended, could spiral into a full-blown mutiny or morale problem. Either way this would not be a good sign. If you did decide to buy the business anyway, you will have to allow for extra time and resources to clean house and replace workers.

3. Lack of organization. If either you or the seller lack organization, this can be overcome by creating a plan.

Deal Breakers

Deal breakers are more serious in nature. They might come as a result of finding information that contradicts statements made by the seller, liabilities that have to be assumed by you that seem extreme, broken commitments, or complications which could put the business at risk or expose you to a level of risk that is unacceptable.

Not every discrepancy is necessarily a deal breaker. It depends on the severity of the discrepancy and the degree of seriousness. There is no book thick enough to cover every possible scenario for every business situation. This is where you earn your stripes as a business owner. You have to make a judgment call and decide for yourself what the implications of the information mean and the actions you will take. However, there are certain issues that I would consider deal breakers. They include:

1. Sloppy bookkeeping or record keeping that does not follow Generally Accepted Accounting Principles (GAAP) that upon an audit might be considered misleading, evasive, or fraudulent.

2. Inability to trace financial transactions throughout the bookkeeping system. For example, I would want to match supplier sales records to what appears in the bookkeeping system. This would also apply to not being able to match purchase orders to supplier invoices. Missing purchase orders often indicate someone is stealing from the business by misrepresenting themselves as a buyer from the company and getting product without paying for it. They indemnify the company in the process.

3. Misrepresentation on the part of the seller. For example, a material misrepresentation of gross or net profit and liabilities that are uncovered and were not disclosed by the seller but were uncovered during a credit check of the business.

4. Departure of key management personnel during the due diligence period to a competitor. This could indicate someone inside the business lacks discretion or is trying to make an end play or set up a business that would dilute the marketplace.

5. Word getting out into the marketplace of the possibility of a change of ownership of the business. A single indiscretion could cause irreparable damage to the business's ability to earn income. For example, the competition hears of the pending deal and begins to cherry-pick key staff, management, and customers.

Overcoming Obstacles and Roadblocks

At some point in this process you are likely going to push the buttons of the seller and he or she may get upset with you. They may even accuse you of being nosy. Tell them they're right. You are being nosy. It is your job to protect your interests and those of your investors or partners. What would they do if they were in your position?

Framing provides a conceptual or contextual "framework and foundation" to facilitate effective two-way communication. Poor communication can often be attributed to differing agendas, viewpoints, or opinions. Each party has their own objectives in attempting to influence the other party.

The purpose of framing is to redirect attention to the subject of the conversation.

The Preframe

The first framing strategy is called a *preframe*. It is usually happens at the beginning of a conversation. Or it is used before attempting to communicate something difficult, to ask for a commitment or a decision, and to effect change. First, we must ensure that we have fertile soil to sow seeds of change

Strategy: First tell them you have something to tell them and that it is important to them. Then tell them why it is important to them. Only after they agree that it is important do you tell them "what" the conversation or issue is all about. In essence we are getting the other party to "emotionally buy-in" before asking them to do or change something.

"When we were talking the other day about your need for a short due diligence period, it started me thinking. I want to discuss what you said and the impact it would have. You might not be happy with what I have to say but I believe that we can come to an agreement."

This is an example of using a preframe to deal with a difficult circumstance. Basically, I warned the seller that I wanted to revisit our discussion and that he would not like what I had to say. Then all I have left to do is start the discussion by reviewing what he said, then telling him why it would not work. Then I tell him what I need and ask him if he can live with that.

This is an excellent method to get someone to come around to your point of view. It just requires a little preparation to decide how you want to preframe the issue (or warn them).

The Reframe

The *reframe* is used to redirect the focus of attention and direction back onto the conversation. The key here is to be stubborn. If you really believe it, stick it out!

Strategy: The primary tactic is to redirect their attention. Either by moving them away from their position through helping them see something unpleasant or move them toward your idea through something you know they really want. Use analogies or metaphors to draw comparisons of your idea and explain it in terms the hearer can understand.

For example, I am in a meeting with the seller and the discussion is way off topic and he has raised the issue of a short timeline for the due diligence period. We had an agreement to a 30-day period, and I am going to hold him to it. "Bringing that up again after we had come to an agreement on a 30-day period is your choice. Rather than sit here discussing that again let's move on to the task at hand so we can both make some money."

Whenever you use a framing technique, simply move on with their implied acceptance regardless of their reaction. In the case of a reframe we use a startling statement combined with another statement to refocus their attention back onto the topic at hand, something they care about. In this case, I spoke about making money. It is something he can move toward without my having to take a hard line on his keeping his word.

The Deframe

The purpose of a *deframe* is to totally interrupt and stop a particular conversational pattern or line of thought.

Strategy: Make a startling statement. Go for the shock value if you have to. The idea is to make absolutely sure that you get their undivided attention. Then move on to what you want to discuss, do, or accomplish. The deframe is very powerful and you really have to be sure that you are committed to using it with confidence; otherwise do not attempt it.

Think of the deframe as a signal interrupt. It works like changing tracks on a railroad. One moment you are heading one direction and suddenly you are going in a completely different direction. It interrupts them by getting their attention with a totally different topic. So I am in a meeting with the seller, and he is constantly being interrupted by phone calls and people walking into his office; finally I have had enough and say, "I want to show you something. Come with me." Then I get up and go somewhere private to show him something in the business I want to discuss. I simply take him there and begin to show him the item and ask a series of questions. When the time is right I suggest that we should find somewhere private where we can talk in confidence and where we will not be interrupted.

A deframe only works if it is strong enough to interrupt their pattern to catch them off guard, then you simply lead them to the topic at hand. You have to be willing to think on your feet and look very determined. It is one of the most powerful ways to lead people in a difficult situation.

19

Finding Solutions and Preparing a Letter of Intent

Eventually you and the seller will come to some sort of agreement. It will involve specifics and generalities. Needless to say, a lot of information will have passed between you and the seller during negotiations. Putting it down on paper is designed to protect both parties. The document should include the price, conditions, terms, and commitments of each party that are open to negotiation prior to signing a final contract.

Disclaimer: This text is not legal advice, simply the opinions and views of the author. You are solely responsible for all actions, decisions, and outcomes that result from conclusions you make as a result of reading this book.

TIP

Seek legal counsel before signing any legal agreement.

The Letter of Intent

Once you have made a determination that the business is worth buying, it is time to think about your letter of intent. At this point in the negotiation process the buyer and seller have come to an agreement on the price, conditions, and terms.

A letter of intent is also referred to as an offer to purchase, memorandum of understanding (MOU), letter of understanding (LOI), or memorandum of agreement.

What the document is called is not as important as understanding what it is, what it does, and why it is used.

What It Is

The letter of intent is simply a document that lists the price, conditions, and terms under which you, the buyer, are willing to purchase the business.

What It Does

A letter of intent or offer to purchase is a written contract that, when accepted by the seller, forms a legally binding contract subject to the terms and conditions stated in the document. It sets out a specific period of time to allow you to inspect the business, records, and government compliance.

Why It Is Used

At a point in the negotiation process the buyer and seller come to an agreement on the price, conditions, and terms, and these are laid out in the letter of intent. However, a business is a complicated entity. Success and failure are determined by a number of interrelated and dependent factors.

During the negotiations representations are made by both the seller and the buyer, and each agrees to a limited period of time to allow the buyer to properly inspect the business. This time period can range between 10 working days (which I do not recommend) and 20 working days or more. This is the period of due diligence, and it is the buyer's opportunity to obtain documentation from the seller to verify that the representations made are accurate and fairly represent the true situation, health, and condition of the business.

What It Often Contains

A letter of intent or offer to purchase provides the parties with a binding agreement that covers negotiations, confidentiality, noninfringement of third-party rights, and also the main terms that do not become binding until the execution of the final agreement. Important content often included are:

- Negotiation deadline
- Termination of the letter of intent
- Description of the potential for a final agreement and terms
- Location of litigation in case of dispute

It also allows the buyer to inspect the business and assets and speak with suppliers and staff.

TIP

Even with the best intentions on both sides, a dispute can easily arise. I highly recommend including a clause to bind the parties to arbitration to resolve any disputes.

Do Not Use Templates

Do not under any circumstances sign a letter of intent without first reviewing it with your attorney or lawyer. Any template you use will have general legal terms and should only be used as a guide to familiarize yourself with the structure, layout, and terms. Samples should never be used as a contract for your deal. If the legal and business language is too broad, you would in fact increase your risk and a court could find that the contract was binding. Get an attorney to create your letter of intent.

TIP

If a business is worth buying, it is worth doing right, and that means protecting yourself. Hire an attorney.

Binding Provisions

The exact provisions and clauses of your letter of intent will be determined through a discussion of your specific situation by you and your attorney. Some of the provisions that are included:

- The buyer and seller agree to deal exclusively. As the buyer you will not pursue any other opportunities and the seller will not entertain other buyers or accept another letter of intent.
- Buyer agrees to return all confidential materials.
- The buyer typically agrees to the nonsolicitation of employees should the purchase not proceed.
- Each party has a duty to negotiate in good faith. Good faith happens when each party discloses and truly represents every material circumstance relating to the letter of intent and makes legitimate and honest efforts to meet obligations in a given situation.

Nonbinding Provisions

Because negotiations are not over, the letter of intent should list provisions that are nonbinding. This can include but not be limited to the purchase price, payment terms, method of valuation, and mutual consent to hire a specific business valuator. Other nonbinding provisions could include exclusion of specific assets as determined by the buyer. This could allow the buyer to exclude certain pieces of equipment, building, or assets from the deal. For example, the buyer would be able to reconsider buying a building if the buyer was to find a better location or the price was too high. Make sure to include as many items as you anticipate needing to renegotiate.

Other Considerations

An important clause to include is one that allows you to work in the business until the closing of the final sale date. I would also consider including some sort of bailout clause should you find discrepancies during this period. It could provide you with a much-needed back door to release you from the commitments you made in the agreement.

TRAP

Find out if there are other contracts such as leasing agreements, employment contracts, and licensing agreements. If other contracts exist, you will want to know their terms before signing a buy-sell agreement.

You should also consider including in the agreement responsibility for any pending lawsuits over wrongful dismissal that could be passed on to a new owner. Consider whether there are any environmental concerns. Are there any tax audits? If so, make audited tax returns a part of the seller's obligations. Part of the proceeds of the sale could be placed in trust for a specific period of time. If a lawsuit or tax audit actually happens that involves actions by the previous owner, that money can be used to fund a defense. But this would need to be spelled out in the buy-sell agreement.

Consider getting a noncompetition agreement from the seller. While these can be difficult to enforce depending on the terms, it should protect you from the seller's opening up a new shop just a few doors away from the one sold to you. It would be important to clearly identify the amount you are paying for the noncompetition agreement, so that you can deduct this amount (for tax purposes) against the ordinary income of the business over the life of the agreement. Depending on where you live and work, these laws can vary greatly. It is worthwhile to investigate and educate yourself. Your attorney can incorporate this into the letter of intent.

Depending on whether you are buying shares or assets of the business, your letter of intent will be substantially different. A purchase of shares requires a lot more work to be done in the due diligence stage because of the potential for unwanted liabilities. If you are simply purchasing the equipment, the process is a much simpler and the agreement will reflect that.

TIP

Specific considerations for a particular industry and type of business could and should be included in the contract.

When drafting the letter of intent, you need to include stipulations about representations made by the owner, e.g., taxes being paid. This will ensure that you are not buying a business with a hidden time bomb like several years of back taxes that will cause a massive bill when you take ownership. It is also very important that the seller guarantee that the company's assets are not encumbered by liabilities and all outstanding bills have been paid.

Preparation Checklist

At this point in the process you enter the research phase, where you use your five senses to examine the company. This is more than just looking at the financial statements. In fact, you will want to familiarize yourself with every aspect of the business. Once you have begun discussions with the seller, the following questions will help you get ready to finalize the deal:

- Have you written down your goals, boundaries, and decision-making parameters? Are they specific and measurable and do they indicate a due date?

- Have you prepared blank nondisclosure agreements? If you have begun discussions with someone already and do not have a confidentiality agreement in place, get one signed right away. I would get each employee to also sign a nondisclosure agreement.

- If you have reached an agreement to buy the business, have you put your intent in writing by using a letter of intent or a formal offer to purchase agreement? Did you do it yourself or use an attorney? If you did it yourself, get it reviewed by an attorney.

- Are the financial statements accurate? Are there any unrealized liabilities? For example, are there any outstanding environmental cleanup or compliance issues, past litigation, or outstanding judgments?

- Is this a good candidate to buy? How do you feel about the viability of the company?

- As for the company's assets, do you have a complete list? What is the value of these assets? Does your valuation agree with the financial statements?

- Is the company's inventory in good condition? Is it resalable? What percentage is not saleable?

- Have you spoken to customers? How do they feel about the company? What would they want to improve?

- Are there any contracts the company has that will or will not continue under new ownership?

- Is the business profitable or is it losing money? Do you see any opportunity to boost revenues and profits?

- How would you describe the mood of the staff and sales team?

- How competitive is the industry? What is the general financial health of the industry? How does that compare to the company you are thinking of buying?

- How would you describe the company's market position?

- Based upon what you have learned, does the business have a viable future?

- Have you prepared your net worth statement?

- Have you reviewed your credit report recently?

- How far are you willing to compromise before you cut your losses and abandon buying this particular business? What things will kill the deal?

- Have you defined roles for professional advisers (accountant, business broker, attorney, etc.)?

- Do you have fixed-price service contracts with professional advisers?

- Do you have a friend or family member you can rely on for independent, unbiased support?

Advanced Communication Tips

How People Evaluate Proposals

In a sense a letter of intent is a proposal. Understanding how people evaluate a proposal will help you when it comes time to put your letter of intent on the table.

We evaluate things, people, and situations based upon either an internal or external frame of reference or context. If you understand what frame of reference a seller is using when evaluating your letter of intent, you can be more effective when communicating by aligning with the seller's context or frame of reference.

Internally Motivated

Internally motivated people evaluate things based upon what they think. They provide their own motivation and want to make their own decisions. They are often perceived as stubborn and find it difficult to accept direction from other people. They might ask you for your opinion, but do not mistake that for their asking for your assistance in making a decision, they will still want to make up their own mind.

Tell them, "It's up to you, only you can decide what is right for you." Align with them being in control because there is nothing you can say or do to change their mind. What you can do is ask them why they feel that way or to "share their experience with you."

External Motivation

Externally motivated people do things because of what they perceive other people think. They have difficulty deciding for themselves. They want to know what other people think, what the experts say, who else is has made a similar decision, and whether or not the decision is popular.

You can direct these people by sharing stories of what other people have done in a similar circumstance.

The next time you speak with a seller, customer, or employee, look for the things they say and the way they say it. If you listen carefully, they will reveal whether they are externally or internally motivated. Just pose a question like, "How do you know that?" If they answer, "I just know it from practical experience," or state, "It just makes sense," then you can be fairly certain that they are motivated by an internal frame of reference. If they make a reference to something someone said or something they saw someone do, they are likely externally motivated.

20

Due Diligence— Verifying Information

The purpose of the due diligence phase is to confirm statements and claims made by the seller and also to confirm that the numbers you used to make your decision are accurate. (On the basis of your accountant's review of the financials, you will be able to redo your valuations based on actual figures, if they differ at all from the information used previously.)

TIP

The due diligence phase is not the time to decide if the business is worth buying. You should have already made that decision before getting to this point. Due diligence allows you to get factual information to back up and verify everything that was said in negotiations.

If you've been keeping notes in meetings with the seller, it's likely that there will be things you want to check out during this time. Often a seller will make a statement in passing that strikes you as odd or out of context. Now is your chance to follow up on it. Independent verification is important because representations made by the seller become assumptions you use to do your analysis and make a decision to proceed. These can include representations made about profit margins, sales, and supplier arrangements.

Take the Time to Verify Everything

In Appendix C I provide a due diligence checklist with 19 categories of information that should be researched and investigated during this phase in the business buying process. Each category can have 10 or more specific items to check and verify. That would mean nearly 200 separate pieces of information to be acquired!

You should make sure that you allow at least 20 working days (one month) to conduct an effective due diligence examination. You will be surprised how quickly the time will go by.

TRAP

Make sure to leave yourself an ample amount of time for due diligence. Small businesses are usually not very well organized, and it will take longer to get your hands on the information you need.

Prepare a List of Required Materials

The preparation checklist from Chapter 19 will help you prepare a list of all the materials required to conduct each aspect of the due diligence process. Make sure your attorney includes the items you identified in Chapter 19 and the materials required in your letter of intent or offer to purchase agreement.

The Clock Starts When . . .

Now it's time to meet with the seller and explain what you will be doing and what you will need. This is also the time to explain the amount of time you need to conduct your due diligence, 20 working days, or one month.

Explain that the due diligence period does not start until you are in receipt of all the materials requested. Negotiate a timeline with the seller of when you can expect to pick up the materials you listed. Reinforce that the 20-day period does not begin *until* you have everything.

I think you can begin to see that preparing in advance is essential. You will also need to monitor progress every day. Make sure that whomever you hire to be your helper (whether friend or family member), expects to have his or her work checked daily to monitor progress or roadblocks.

TIP

Not being organized when you begin the due diligence phase is only going to increase your risk of missing something. Break the tasks down by department (sales, accounting, employees, assets, etc). Keep a separate list for each. As each task is completed, cross it off the list. Keep the "to do" list current. You will be able to focus better if you eliminate completed items, and you can continually monitor the remaining work to determine if any changes have to be made.

Obviously, this cannot be done quickly and will take time. To repeat, do not let the seller push you for a 10-day due diligence period. This process should take at least 30 to 45 days which gives you a chance to experience a complete billing cycle and get to know staff, suppliers, and customers.

Due Diligence List of Lists

The due diligence checklist that appears in Appendix C should only be used as a guideline. I have purposely not created a checklist for each and every area of a business because there are so many different types of businesses that providing a master checklist would only increase your risk of missing something. It is important for you to create your own checklist, one that is specific to the business you are seeking to buy. By creating your own list you will be pleasantly surprised by how the process imbeds the information into your memory. This is something that no preformatted list or template could possibly provide. You will be better prepared and better able to think on your feet, too.

TIP

In Chapter 18 I discussed organizing your notes into spreadsheets to create your own lists of the resources and documents needed. Use these lists as a basis for your due diligence checklist.

Having said this about the value and importance of making your own checklists, in order to give you some help getting started, here is my list of lists and tasks that need to be investigated in eight areas that apply to most businesses.

Employees

- You will need a list of employees, including the seller.

- Review employee resumes, job applications, and employee file. Everyone who applies for a job lists their previous employers, and if they came from within the industry, the information can be valuable in providing names of competition, background, and work history of the employees.

- Ask for employee human resource (HR) files. Reviewing staff HR files will also give you a sense of how they have been dealt with. If there are no written HR records, then ask the owner to sit down with you to discuss each employee history, performance, and observations.

- Check job applications and resumes for accuracy. Especially if they were not checked in the first place. There are companies that will do a background check and verify references for about $500. If people appear to have advanced degrees and they do not, you have to wonder what else they might be lying about.

- Make sure you know the laws in your jurisdiction regarding what you cannot ask about in an interview and while checking references.

- Ask for or acquire information about the privacy laws/rights in your area. For example, inquiries about medical history, arrest records, and former drug use are illegal; under federal law.

- Start learning about key staff. Ask the seller which employee he could not do without and why. What would the consequences be to the business? Have the seller put actual numbers to the cost of the employee leaving—real numbers. I heard the story of a company that when confronted by this question realized that if their engineer left it could realistically cost them $29,000,000! Immediately the owner wrote the engineer a check for $1,000,000—a lot cheaper than if the employee left. If you agree with the seller's assessment, make sure this employee stays with you. Find out the person's goals and what ideas she or he might have for the business. To make sure the employee stays, consider an immediate reward or bonus, which will make sure the employee cannot be lured away by a competitor. Also make sure to get key employees to sign a nondisclosure agreement. Once the word is out on the street that the business is for sale, competitors may try to cherry-pick the staff.

- Do you understand the local labor markets? In a tight labor market, your options for tightening benefits will be limited. In a tight labor market, opportunities abound for employees, and this makes them more sensitive to changes in benefits, remuneration, and working conditions. So be cautious and make sure you are aware of the market conditions and think through how this could affect your human resource decisions.

- What is the makeup of the management and staff? Based on how you plan to run the business, what changes would you like to make? What gaps exist? Do job descriptions currently exist? How would you change the job descriptions and overall staff makeup?

- Do you have a backup list of job seekers that you can turn to if needed? Do some form of preliminary background screening. Do you have a commitment from the manager to stay with you? How would losing him or her affect time-to-market, image, and sales volumes for the next two to three years? How badly would this manager's leaving disrupt the team? What if the person left and went to your main competitor?

- Does the business have the right people but just have them in the wrong position? Make a list of changes you would need to make.

- Labor relations: Are all benefits, i.e., workers' compensation, health benefits, and pension plans (if any) current and up to date? Check with the insurance company to see what the claim rate experience for employee benefits is and if there are any pending or recent increases in insurance premiums?

- Is there a sales team? How are they doing? Turnover? Are the company's products or services a one-time sale or are there repeat orders? What types of sales training programs have been used? How are they using technology? What is the morale of the sales team? Are they paid according to industry standards?

- Request a monthly sales report for the last 12 months and annual reports for the previous two years. If there is a sales team involved, who is making the majority of sales? If it is the owner, what will that mean when you take over the business? Why is the owner the best salesman? If an employee is the best salesperson, will that person stay with you, and what can you learn about the business from that person? Is the compensation fair or inflated? Are the salespeople being overpaid? If there is a sales team, how are you going to manage it? Are you experienced and capable of managing it? If not, where will you get a sales manager and how much will it cost? If a sales manager is already employed, do you want to keep him or her? Is there a need for a change? If so, do you have a replacement?

Operations

- Depending on the type of business you are buying, you will need to keep an open mind about the way the operation is managed.

- Look at the factors that affect core operations. Are they adequately resourced and staffed? If not, what needs to be changed or added?

- Is the equipment in good operating condition? Make a list of equipment, serial numbers, age, etc.

- What is the value of the equipment? Are replacement parts available?

- Which equipment is owned, which is leased? Check the condition of equipment.

- How long will you be able to make money with that equipment in current condition?

- Is a warranty available and transferable? Is the manufacturer still in business and able to provide parts?

- How much maintenance will be required per year, and would it be cheaper to replace it? If you had to replace the equipment, what is the current replacement cost? Can you afford to replace it? Check the financial statements to see how much the current owner has depreciated the equipment.

- Look at systems that are in place, how well are they working? Ask staff for their feedback.

Assets

- Building: Check the zoning bylaws to confirm compliance with development and civic building codes. In some communities there are special caveats and restrictions on commercial development. I saw a business that operated for 16 years without a problem, and 3 years after the new owner was running the business, he got a notice that the layout and use of the property did not comply with a specific code. He had 45 days to submit a new plan for redevelopment.

- If you are buying the building, make sure you get a real estate appraisal.

- If you are leasing the property and building, check to make sure that the lease is transferable. Otherwise you could end up with a business and no legal right to occupy the space. Check with the property owner and get a letter in writing.

Review Liabilities

- Your purpose here is to verify any obligations that you will be assuming when you take over the business. For example, do the business records match the supplier records? I once worked with an automotive repair shop whose profits seemed unusually low. By looking at supplier records and matching parts purchased to work orders, we uncovered that there were missing work orders and eventually figured out that the owner had been taking customer cash payments for work orders and putting it into his pocket.

- Your accountant will verify that government taxes have been accurately reported and paid. Request copies of any agreements or contracts so your attorney can review any contracts that you will be assuming. Get a current list of accounts payable and supplier statements and copies of all bank accounts, leases, loans, and lines of credit. Is the business compliant with workers' compensation and local labor laws? Have there been any legal judgments against the corporation or owner? If so, discuss the implications with your attorney.

Customers

- Review customer purchases and identify the top 20 percent of customers and ask for meetings to be set up. The seller will likely be reluctant to provide that access and want to restrict your research to a review of past purchases. In these business-to-business situations the following strategy is easy to implement and addresses the concerns of the seller. Have the seller or a salesman introduce you as a management trainee who is going to be sitting in on some meetings.

TIP

Once you complete the sale, go back and introduce yourself and apologize for the intrigue. Explain that you were restricted by the concerns of the owner.

- If you are buying a retail store, you can easily observe the customers and their interactions with staff, and that will give you a good feel for what is really going on.

Suppliers

- What is the history with the suppliers? Are they paid on time? Compare the suppliers' records with the Income Statement supplied by the seller. It is a good idea to request an Aged Trial Balance report. It will provide you with the detail required to trace back any of the transactions you choose.

- Are there written agreements with suppliers? If so, will the right to sell pass to you? If so, get it in writing. If not, you will have to renegotiate with suppliers.

Financial Review

- You and your accountant will review and probe in every financial area. Basically you are looking to verify that the financial statements have an adequate paper trail and that the costs shown are correct. Without this information you will not know for sure what the true profit margins actually are.

- Have any expenses been hidden or what should have been personal expenses debited to the business? Have the financial statements been prepared according to Generally Accepted Accounting Principles (GAAP)? Do the financial statements accurately reflect the true status of the financial health of the business?

- Have there been any changes in assets that were not properly accounted for? For example, selling a piece of equipment and allocating it to general revenue has the effect of inflating the revenue and profit margins.

- What part of the business is growing and which is slipping? Why is this happening? Should this change your decision to buy the business?

- Banking: Review all bank statements. What accounts do they have? Do they use lines of credit? If so, how are they used and what are interest rates? What type of security does the bank hold? Inventory, assets, and accounts receivable? Has the owner signed a general security agreement, i.e., a promissory note to suppliers or banks? Will the bank release the seller once sale is complete and redo the agreements?

- Inventory report: you will require a complete inventory of all equipment, tools, and small parts that will be included in the deal. Plus any exceptions should be noted in writing. Check the report for fair valuation. If there is any question as to the value, hire an independent appraiser to place a value on the inventory. Remember, this inventory report may become a part of your agreement so accuracy is crucial.

Legal Issues

- The most obvious legal issue will be your offer to purchase or letter of intent, due diligence agreement, and final sales agreement. If the seller is staying with you under a management contract, obviously you will want to have your attorney prepare a rock-solid contract complete with a non-competition agreement. Your attorney will likely have a checklist that he uses and may provide you with it to use as a guide.

- One of the important areas to check into will be of an environmental nature. You will want to make sure that you determine whether there are any environmental issues that create liability for the corporation such as spills or outstanding site cleanup that would be needed when the property is sold. This is especially important if you are doing a stock purchase. Make sure that the seller carries the burden for cleanup and compliance of any environmental issues before you take over. If you let them promise to do it later, even if it is in writing and they do not do it, you will still be the one held responsible.

- Make sure to request copies of all outstanding contracts. Are there any supplier contracts? If so, will they continue to sell to you? Get it in writing, as sometimes these contracts do not automatically survive the sale of a business; some can require prior approval. Check to see if there are any written agreements or contracts with employees, especially managers. Are there noncompetition agreements in place with management? If not, you should have your attorney make one up if you buy the business. Make sure that the business is current on all contracts and obligations.

Create Your Acquisition Plan

During the due diligence period make time to write your acquisition or business plan. Take everything you have learned about the business and begin to play with the numbers on the pro forma financial projections.

21
Executing a Deal

Buying with Confidence—
Review Your Work

Making a deal is all about confidence. At this point you have spent at least one month conducting a due diligence inspection, not to mention all the soul searching and research discussed at the beginning of this book.

If you do not feel confident at this point, do not proceed. Take time to review all your notes and what you discovered during the due diligence process. Have you discovered anything that you cannot live with? It is one thing to be nervous—after all it is a big decision—but it is quite another to have a valid reason (material misrepresentation, etc., by the seller) to not buy the business. Here are some questions to help you look at things afresh:

1. Can you be profitable and repay your debts if you owned this business? What do your financial projections show? If you show a profit, have you done a sensitivity analysis to see how much profit there would be if your costs increased and sales dropped? Have you planned for a drop in revenue for the first three to six months of the transition?

2. What was the main reason you decided to pursue buying this business? Has that reason changed? Were you able to uncover any information that confirmed your initial decision to buy this business?

3. What is the five-year outlook for this industry? How does the market look over the next five years? Where are the new opportunities?

4. If there are new opportunities in the market, how do you plan to make the most of these opportunities? How much would these new opportunities add to your revenue?

5. How do your pro forma financial projections compare to the industry? Are your sales, profits, and balance sheet comparable? Where are your pro forma projections better than average, and what plans do you have to implement these projections?

6. In your discussions with your accountant or CPA what were his or her comments? How did those comments affect your decision and desire to buy this business?

7. Were you able to speak with the company's best customers? Do you expect to be able to retain their business? Did you uncover any unmet needs that you could use to strengthen your position? If so, what would be the net contribution to your overall revenue and profit position?

8. What is the morale of the employees and management? Who do you feel you will be able to lean on for additional support and assistance in the early days? If there is a sales team, how are they feeling about the potential for new management? Do you have a plan for them to make the most of the first 90 days?

9. When you spoke with the suppliers did you think they could help you in making the transition? Is there inventory or equipment they can help you clean out or update?

10. When you looked at the operations and systems did you see any areas of improvement you wanted to make? If so, do you have the support of the employees? Do they see it as a positive move forward?

11. In your financial review and pro forma projections were you able to identify opportunities to reduce overhead or costs? If so, how much in net savings would that amount to in the first year?

12. Were you able to get the owner to agree to provide consulting services to assist you and provide you with training?

As you review your answers to the 12 questions above, what is the trend? Do you see more positive outcomes in your answers? If there are no deal breakers uncovered while answering these questions, you feel more positive as a result, and your business plan holds up under scrutiny, then you are in good shape to achieve your goals.

TIP

It is natural to feel nervous and have doubts. Making a decision takes only a moment, justifying the decision and feeling comfortable with it is something that happens over time. As you get into operating the business, the doubts and nervousness will fade.

How People Make Decisions

Making a decision is quick. It happens in a moment. But getting ready to make a decision can take a long time. Understanding how people make decisions can help in communicating with them more effectively and help them arrive at a decision faster.

People make decisions because it either looks right, feels right, sounds right, or makes sense to them. We often tell ourselves we make decisions based upon logic and reason, but often a decision is an emotional one that we justify with logic.

"Looks Right People" make decisions based upon how they see a picture in their minds of how it literally looks right. They like examples or graphs, etc. Show them pictures; paint them a mental picture with words. They trust what they can see.

"Sounds Right People" do things because they hear a series of words which sound right to them. They like to hear about things. Tell them about your product; pay attention to your voice intonation to ensure it shows confidence and sincerity.

"Feels Right People" make decisions best by trying the product out so they can get a good feeling about it. They literally feel a sensation in their body that feels right.

"Makes Sense People" need reasons for what you want them to do that makes sense. Give them facts, data, and reasons. Answer the "why" for them. They use information in a way that produces a feeling that makes sense to them.

Communication Tips

Listen for obvious conversational clues. Listen for key phrases in your conversation "Well that makes sense to me!" or "Looks OK to me." Another is "Oh, that feels good!"

By listening to what people say, asking questions, and observing their behaviors, they will literally tell you how they go about making a decision, and you will be able to tell when they have made a decision.

When in Doubt Refer Back to the Letter of Intent

Your letter of intent outlines items that are binding and those that are non-binding, which, depending on your letter of intent, can be renegotiated.

A written offer can be accepted only in writing. The terms of your letter of intent and how it is structured will determine how things will proceed. Sometimes the agreement will state that when a payment is made this could be considered either an "absolute acceptance" or "conditional acceptance." A conditional acceptance is good only when some condition occurs or a change to the original agreement is accepted.

The Final Sales Agreement

Be prepared to provide your attorney with instructions on how you want to proceed and ask the attorney for feedback. Communicate any changes or departures from the letter of intent that the seller and you have made.

If you have done the work as described throughout this book, this stage will not be intimidating to you. It will simply be another step in the process.

TIP

Your attorney is best qualified to guide you through this part of the process. When in doubt refer back to the letter of intent because it outlines the price, conditions, and terms of what was agreed to and what your next steps will be. Let your attorney lead and guide you through the execution of the final agreements.

Now is the time to begin making the transition. Take some time to celebrate, go out for dinner, and talk about the journey you have been on. Voice what you have learned to those closest to you. Congratulations, you are on an exciting journey!

22

The Transition: Making the Business Yours and Boosting Morale

The First 90 Days

To make sure that you do not experience a drop in revenue after the change in management, you will need a plan. You will need to be well organized and maintain a razor sharp focus.

TRAP

Most small businesses *do* experience a drop in revenue after a change in management. Smart planning and organization will help you to avoid this trap.

After assuming management and operational control, you need to send a clear message to the employees, suppliers, and your customers. They need to know you are in charge and what your plans are for the business. Most important, they will need to know how they fit into your plans.

This is a unique opportunity in the life of a business. You will never again have the same chance to set the tone for your style of leadership and to establish your brand. The impact this can have on marketing and sales in the first 90 days is significant. To take advantage of this opportunity, you need a communication plan with detailed tasks, including an implementation timeline.

What Is a Communication Plan?

A communication plan is a deliberate and targeted approach to transmitting information with the overall goal of satisfying the curiosity of customers, suppliers, and employees. The goal is to deliver a balanced message that provides peace of mind and creates excitement about the future of the business. A communication plan includes the following elements:

1. *Who.* Define which group or individual you wish to communicate with: employees, customers, or suppliers. What is important to them?

2. *Result.* Why are you communicating with them? Define your goals. What do you want to accomplish as a result of your communication?

3. *Message.* What do you need them to know? As it relates to buying the business, what do they care about most? What is the message you need them to hear?

4. *Method and Tools.* How are you going to go about communicating with them? There will be situations that are best handled face to face and other times when a letter will do. Which tools will you utilize to get the message across? What will get their attention?

5. *Test for Success.* Define how you will measure success. A communication plan is dynamic. You will get feedback. It is essential to learn from this feedback. It is important to determine, in advance, how you will define success, and what you will do if your efforts fail. You must be prepared for a certain amount of failure. People are distracted and it may take more than a few tries before they get the message that accomplishes your goals. Being able to shift and make adjustments is important.

A Morale Boost

TIP

Prior to having a general staff meeting, meet with key employees and management to communicate your plans for the first 90 days and your expectations of them. Set a series of goals for the first two weeks, and assign responsibilities and due dates.

After meeting with key employees and management, set up a short staff meeting to thank them for their cooperation and the assistance they provided to help you get to this point. State your goals for the first 90 days and include revenue targets as well as changes you want to make to the facility.

For example, put up a fresh coat of paint, move desks, furniture, or equipment, and tell them you plan to meet with them all individually over the next couple of weeks. Ask them to start thinking about what they need to do their job that they currently do not have. Make it clear that not all requests will be acted upon immediately but that they will be discussed and put into the company's overall plan, as soon as possible. Low-cost renovations and improvements will lift their spirits and is a positive, visible sign that things are changing.

Seller's Remorse

If the seller is staying on to help with the transition, you will need to set clear boundaries to prevent confusion. Explain that your desire is for the seller to take a supportive role and direct all enquiries that normally would have been dealt with by him or her, to you. Ask the seller to stay in the background and explain that this is your time to make your mark on the business and earn the trust and respect of all staff, customers, and suppliers.

TIP

Let the seller know that you understand that this time may feel awkward for everyone and that he made a quality decision to sell the business, and you appreciate his support during this stressful time.

When a seller goes from being at the center of attention and knowing everything that is going on in the business, to being an outsider, there will be withdrawal symptoms. It will not be perfect and the seller may forget that he or she is no longer the owner. When this happens make a mental note, and if it continues and becomes an ongoing issue, sit down to discuss and resolve this conflict.

One of the ways of preventing confusion is to develop job descriptions for everyone including yourself and the previous owner. Write these down. You can then point out the piece of paper that outlines the previous owner's new responsibilities. This shifts the focus to the piece of paper and the job description, not the person.

Five Qualities of Effective Managers When Taking over Management

It is the manager's job to provide tools, resources, and systems to intermediate the supply and demand process. An effective manager:

1. Asks more questions than gives advice.

2. Always believes in the staff and trains staff versus simply telling them what he or she expects.

3. Provides clear and honest communication.

4. Sets the vision of the company, worthwhile goals, and establishes corporate values. The manager sets standards and expectations of performance for the company, managers, and staff.

5. Creates a positive environment where respect is shown for people's differences. The manager provides support, feedback, understanding, and encouragement.

An effective manager in today's business environment carries a combination of roles, including teacher, coach, and motivator. And of course the authority of being in charge; however, the most important role is that of leader. A leader that lives a life of integrity, displays humility, and does not try to control the outcome of everything.

Powerful leaders are committed to their people and project authority but do not lord it over the staff. He or she displays confidence and the ability to make decisions that meet company objectives. He is able to adequately resource the business and deal with performance issues quickly. He rewards honesty and accepts criticism. Sometimes she leads; often she allows others, within the company, to lead and she follows. He knows how to balance staying out of the way and yet knows when to step in and is willing to make a decision.

Tips for Managing the Previous Owner as an Employee

The first thing to remember is that the seller was an entrepreneur first. He or she will now have to learn how to be an employee or consultant.

Beware of Your Bias and Judgment of the Previous Owner. Previous owners are used to having their own way and have always been very focused on their own agendas. It is an important attribute, because they have an innate ability to see things other people do not see. Now they have to focus on someone else's agenda: yours. Be open to the fact that they might see a problem and solution ahead of you. Listen to their comments and suggestions, then think about them and decide what you want to do.

Accept That the Previous Owner Thinks Differently. Truth is, right away you will need to create adequate controls and procedures to ensure the ongoing viability of the business. Make sure the seller knows exactly what your expectations are of him or her. Explain that you need time to adapt to leading, managing, and controlling business processes, assets, and employees.

Ask the previous owner to speak to you if she really feels that something needs to be dealt with and it will be considered. You might also task the previous owner the job of finding a solution. Let him tinker and experiment. You might be pleasantly surprised with what gets created.

Learn How to Work with the Previous Owner.   There is no doubt that managers and entrepreneurs are wired differently. If the previous owner is more of an entrepreneur and you are more of a manager, temper your frustration by reminding yourself that this employee has a strong entrepreneurial drive. Learn how to put that entrepreneurial drive to work for you.

TIP

There will be a natural tension between you and the seller after you take over the business. Tension, by its nature, seeks resolution. Use dialogue and negotiation as a tool to gain a greater understanding of the seller's ideas, and the tension will melt away.

Do not confuse being in a dialogue with having to agree on every point. Work together. You will learn to appreciate one another and begin to see each other as valuable partners instead of adversaries.

From Corporate Culture to a Sense of Community

Just as the assembly line revolutionized manufacturing, we must change our thinking to revolutionize business. A business is not a machine. It is a community—a community of people who are looking for a meaningful work life in a world of overwork and distraction.

People look to work to provide structure, connection, and a sense of belonging. A business's sustainable competitive advantage is fused with developing staff and tapping into the dynamic and resilient human spirit.

Employees want to feel passionate, connected, and trusted. They want their work to be meaningful. In fact there is a segment of people whose life is focused on "making a difference." The implication for business owners is that they must develop strategies that will create meaning, trust, rapport, inspiration and depth.

Create balance by creating a "sense of community" in the way you manage the business. As the community embraces your business as "part of the community" you get a strong emotional buy-in. This is fragile because as the emotional buy-in grows so do expectations. You own the business, but the community (employees, suppliers, customers) feels a sense of ownership too.

When your business gives a sense of community and rapport to employees, you have:

- Achieved a real, yet intangible sustainable competitive advantage.

- A significant capacity for change while making great strides in efficiency.

- Staff who will demonstrate increased reliability and self-regulation. They move from being managed to being inspired to perform.

This is the new corporate culture that thrives in a service-based economy.

23
Case Studies

Auto Repair Shop

George is a 60-year-old business owner who has run his automotive repair shop for 14 years in an affluent suburban area. George purchased the business from the original owner and has built the business up to over $1.5 million annually. Gross profit averages 45 percent and George takes out around $200,000 per year.

Sam is a dynamic, charismatic 30-something who was working for an automotive jobber as a salesman. George was one of Sam's customers and as they got to know one another Sam recognized that George had built a quality business that enjoyed a strong market position in an affluent area with little competition.

Sam approached George about buying the business. George asked Sam to work for him for a year, learning the business. George would take a two-year vacation while Sam ran the business for him to see if he could handle it. George continued to run the financial side of the business, wrote checks, and did the bookkeeping. He would check in with Sam every couple of months to see how things were going. During this time the business continued the previous growth pattern with its best year of $1.73 million.

Eventually, they agreed on a formula that would allow Sam to buy the business with nothing down and financed by George. The total price was $1.5 million. George was paid $8,000 per month using a deferred compensation plan prepared by his attorney. Plus he was paid $7,000 per month as rent on the building he owned. Sam also has an option to buy the building and land for $750,000 in the third year.

George had his attorney draft the documents and Sam and his wife signed them, providing a personal guarantee in case the business failed. During this same period real estate development bylaws were changed and the amount of competition in the area increased substantially.

Sam's wife joined the business to do the bookkeeping and manage the administrative side of the business that George had always done. Despite the increased competition in the area the business still managed $1.44 million that first year. But sales continued to drop slowly while costs in the business increased. Workers' compensation premiums doubled and health insurance also doubled.

During this period they started to use the corporate bank account to fund personal health care costs, finance a personal vehicle, and other personal expenses. In the process they drew more personal income from the business than it had in profits. In that same period they started to miss rent payments to George.

With the business now in crisis, George came back to take over the bookkeeping and administrative work provided by Sam's wife. While catching up on six months accounting, George discovered that workers' compensation insurance had lapsed as did the health and group life insurance. Despite the health and group life insurance having lapsed they continued to deduct premiums from the employees. They were also over $30,000 in arrears on 401(k) contributions that had been withheld on behalf of the employees.

Essentially the business was insolvent, but George and Sam agreed to try and get the business back on its feet. It took almost two years and very tight financial management by George, but the business is now current with all its bills and is up for sale again.

What Went Wrong?

- There was no formal business plan after Sam took it over. Marriage, personnel, and family problems plagued the family, and with the additional stress the bookkeeping was allowed to slip. As a result no financial statements had been prepared for over six months.

- Increased competition eroded the company's market share.

- The number of new customers dropped each year as did total revenue. Having not moved fast enough to reduce expenses, the company's reserves eroded to the point the company had to tap into a line of credit at the bank to make payroll.

- George's absence was felt much more than anyone had anticipated. His bookkeeping and financial management expertise allowed the business to continue to grow. Previous financial management by George created a huge gap that Sam was not able to fill after he took over.

- No adjustments were made in marketing and advertising despite the substantial increase in competition.

Successful Business Owner Diversifies

When I first met Ron he was a men's hairstylist working in his brother's barber shop cutting hair. When his brother moved to another city, Ron took the opportunity to buy a hair salon in a major metropolitan mall.

He and his brother purchased the mall hair salon and he ran the business for 10 years. When Ron's brother moved back to the city, he sold the mall salon to his brother and used the proceeds to buy another salon in a different part of the city. After operating this business for 8 years, Ron wanted to stop cutting hair. So he purchased a franchise juice bar, located in the food fair of a major mall.

The idea was that he could buy the franchise, hire a manager, and occasionally check in on it, hoping it would run itself. Unfortunately, it did not work out that way. He could not find the right people and had to spend more time at the juice bar filling in for part-time staff that would not show up for work.

After three months of long hours he realized that things were not going to get better and the business would not be able to run itself; he made the decision to close the business and go back to running his hair salon.

What Went Wrong?

- The first error was expecting that he could buy a franchise and it would basically run itself. Business just does not work that way. Perhaps after a period of running the business he might be able find someone to help him run it, but who aspires to becoming a manager of a juice bar when they grow up?

- The fast-food industry relies on part-time staff to prepare the product and take the cash. These types of business are always hiring staff because the turnover is so high. It does not matter what type of fast-food franchise you buy, they all have the same challenges, finding and training part-time staff.

- These types of businesses are best suited to be run as a family business. Mom and Dad share the workload and the salary. But the business does not run itself. The fact that Ron did not want to work that hard anymore was a clue. He has a better chance of training his hair salon staff to run the business while he keeps an eye on it on a regular basis. He would get the freedom he wants without the need to put in long hours.

Business Dictionary

Accounts payable Money owed to suppliers.

Accounts receivable Money owed by customers.

Accountant One that keeps, audits, and inspects the financial records of individuals or business concerns and prepares financial and tax reports.

Acid-test ratio Can be referred to as the quick ratio; the ratio of current assets minus inventories, accruals, and prepaid items to current liabilities.

Acquisition of assets A merger or consolidation in which an acquirer purchases the selling firm's assets.

Acquisition plan A type of a business plan specifically written to help the buyer make a business decision. Can also be used to help obtain financing.

Acquisition of stock A merger or consolidation in which an acquirer purchases the acquiree's stock.

Articles of incorporation This is a legal document that establishes a corporation and its structure and purpose.

Assets A company's total resources.

Attorney A professional person authorized to practice law; conducts lawsuits or gives legal advice.

Balance sheet Sometimes this is referred to as the statement of financial condition; it is a summary of the assets, liabilities, and owner's equity.

Bankruptcy When a company is unable to pay debts, the ownership of the firm's assets are transferred from the stockholders to the lien holders.

Boilerplate Often used by attorney's or accountants; these are standard terms and conditions. Can also be called a *template*.

Book value A company's total assets minus intangible assets and liabilities, such as debt. A company's book value might be more or less than its fair market value.

Business plan(s) A comprehensive document that discloses the intent of the writer for developing a business. It is usually prepared to assist with gaining financing from a lending institution.

Business risk The risk that the cash flow of a business will be impaired because of adverse economic conditions, making it difficult for the company to meet its operating expenses.

Business valuation An amount in dollars estimated by a qualified appraiser of the value of a company.

Capital expenditures Amount used during a particular period to acquire or improve the long-term assets of the company, such as property, plant, or equipment.

Cash discount This is an incentive offered to purchasers of a company's product for payment within a specified time period, such as 10 days.

Cash flow In a business, it represents cash flow from the normal business operations by sales of the company's products or services. This is important because it indicates the ability to pay dividends.

Collateral Assets than can be repossessed if a borrower defaults.

CPA Certified public accountant who has earned a designation given to an accountant who has passed a national uniform examination and has met other requirements; CPA certificates are issued and monitored by state boards of accountancy or similar agencies.

Debt/equity ratio Indicator of financial leverage. Compares assets provided by creditors to assets provided by shareholders. Determined by dividing long-term debt by shareholder or stockholder equity.

Dividend A dividend is a portion of a company's profit paid to common and preferred shareholders.

Due diligence The investigation of a firm's business to determine whether the firm's business and financial situation and its prospects are adequately disclosed by the seller in the prospectus for the offering.

Earnings Net income for the company during the period.

Equity Represents ownership interest in a firm and the residual dollar value assuming its liquidation.

Fair market value Amount at which an asset would change hands between two parties, both having knowledge of the relevant facts.

Financial plan A financial blueprint for the financial future of a company.

Fixed asset A property owned long term and used by a company in the production of its income. Tangible fixed assets include real estate, plant, and equipment. Intangible fixed assets include patents, trademarks, and customer recognition.

Generally Accepted Accounting Principles (GAAP) A technical accounting term that encompasses the conventions, rules, and procedures necessary to define accepted accounting practice at a particular time.

Goodwill The amount paid by a buyer to the seller of a business that exceeds the value of the assets of the business.

Gross profit margin Gross profit divided by sales. This is also equal to each sales dollar left over after paying for the cost of goods sold.

Hard assets The equipment, inventory, and building/property of a business.

Industry The category describing a company's primary business activity.

Inventory For a company it can include raw materials as well as items available for sale or in the process of being made ready for sale.

Liability A financial obligation or the cash outlay that must be made at a specific time to satisfy the contractual terms of the obligation. The amount owed by a firm to its creditors.

Line of credit An informal and flexible arrangement between a bank and a customer establishing a maximum loan balance that the bank will permit the borrower to maintain.

Marketing The process of communicating with a specific market to offer goods or services for sale.

P&L Profit and loss statement for a company. Can also be called *income statement*.

Pro forma financial statements Financial statements created to reflect a projected or planned set of business transactions.

Product life cycle The time it takes to bring new and/or improved products to market.

Quick ratio Indicator of a company's financial strength (or weakness). Calculated by taking current assets less inventories, divided by current liabilities. This ratio provides information regarding the firm's liquidity and ability to meet its obligations. Can also be called the *acid-test ratio*.

Reorganization Creating a plan to restructure a debtor's business and restore its financial health.

Return on investment (ROI) Generally, income as a proportion of net book value.

Revenue Cash, the result of the sale of a company's products or services.

Risk Typically defined as the deviation of the return on total investment by a company or the degree of uncertainty of return on an asset.

Security Piece of paper that proves ownership of investments.

Shares Certificates representing ownership in a corporation.

Soft assets The intangible, intellectual property, or goodwill in a business.

Stockholder Holder of equity shares in a company.

Stockholders' equity The residual claims that stockholders have against a company's assets, calculated by subtracting total liabilities from total assets.

Takeover General term referring to transfer of control of a firm from one group of shareholders to another group of shareholders.

Taxable income Gross income less a set of deductions.

Appendix **B**

Business Plan
Writing Guide

This is a simplified guide to writing a business plan. It is loosely based on my eBook *The Business Plan Coach* (www.sbishere.com), and it designed to be used with this book as a supplement on how to write a business plan for a business you plan on buying.

TIP

Document your observations of the business (what I refer to in this guide as "before") and then write about the changes you will make after. This will allow you to draw attention to what you are going to do differently, and it also gives you a format to follow when writing the business plan.

Executive Summary

The executive summary is usually written last. It summarizes and provides the reader with an overview. Specifically, you want to include the purchase price of the business, timing, and the two best reasons that this business represents a good investment.

Describe the Business

Here is where you describe the business from two perspectives.

Before: A brief description of the current situation in the business that you plan on buying. It is important to include why the business is for sale, name of the company, corporate structure (proprietorship, corporation, etc.) name of current owner(s), years in business, location, sales volumes, profits.

Construct a timeline (from start-up to today) of the business from date of incorporation to current date that shows the major milestones of the business. Milestones can include sales volume, major events (new shareholders, new products, expansion, etc.).

After: Write a short overview that explains why you are interested in this business, how you found the business (advertising, own research, etc.), big picture of the opportunity (untapped business potential, add new products/services, etc.), your vision for the business, and your goals. You should explain how you plan to alter the legal structure (if any).

Products and Services

Before: Define the profit centers of the business in its current form, including the mix and range of products/services. Include a table that shows the costs and profits by product line and/or services. What the current owner has done to get the business to this point. This should include expansion or growth strategies (if applicable) and products and services that evolved.

Explain the product or service life cycle. Are the products/services sold by the business consumables that get used and repurchased multiple times or are they a one-time sale?

After: Now you have an opportunity to explain the weaknesses and strengths of the current line of products/services. Show how you plan to supplement any products/services and how the overall mix will change the earning potential of the business.

Revise the table from the Before section by adding a column to show the changes this strategy will make to revenues and profits. You should be able to show an increase in both sales and profits because the addition of new products being sold to the existing customer base should always increase revenues and profits.

If the addition of new products/services will also allow you to attract new customers to the business, make sure to point that out as a significant opportunity to use the existing business as a springboard to add a new market and increase market share.

Industry Analysis

Before: If you did the industry research described in Chapter 6 to find the business, you can use that information here.

For the industry as a whole, explain how trends have affected the business and what the business did or did not do to respond to those trends. What is the three- to five-year outlook (demand) for the industry in your area? If this is different than the national trend, then it will be important to point that out in your comments.

If this business was a start-up, explain the barriers faced in starting a business in this industry and specifically how this impacted the current business. Include specific barriers and how these issues have prevented the business from really succeeding or what the current owner did that allowed it to overcome these barriers and perform.

Document the history of the business relating to technology and innovation. Include in your comments how innovation and technology has either helped or hindered this business. For example, the cost of implementing a computerized process and control system can prevent a business from making the initial but important investment.

Include comments about the impact that the economy has had on the business as well as government regulations and the general industry financial health. These external factors can be important to identify especially if they tend to have a direct impact on revenue, productivity, or profits.

After: All the bad news relating to the industry is detailed in the Before section; now is your opportunity to explain how you plan to cope with these issues.

If you identified specific barriers to growth and expansion, provide specific details on how you plan to overcome these barriers or how buying this business will allow you to overcome those barriers. Use a table to show the barriers and issues and then in the next column provide a brief explanation of your plan to offset any negative impact or how you will use these situations as opportunities to grow and expand.

Updating technology in a business can bring about increased productivity and profits. Many industries have gained substantial improvements in productivity and profits from implementing or updating to new technology. If this is applicable in your industry, explain what changes you plan and how you expect that these changes will increase productivity and profits. This one reason alone can be a great reason to buy an established business because technological improvements will only increase the productivity and profits on the entire customer base.

External factors like the economy, competition, and government regulations can be significant in some industries, and if your industry is impacted by these factors, include your strategy to offset them.

If the financial health of the business is a challenge as it is for the industry, spending some time talking about how you plan to overcome these problems will be an important factor contributing to the success of your new venture.

Market Analysis

Before: Show how your local market is the same or different from the industry. Use information from your industry analysis to draw comparisons to the local market the business operates within. If the business is in better shape than the industry, explain how you arrived at that conclusion and what the business has done differently.

Explain the competitive environment and how competitive the business is in this market. Note any weaknesses and strengths in the business's ability to compete. Calculate the current market size and market share that the business currently enjoys.

After: Describe how you plan to compete in the market and what you will do differently. Explain what you know about the market including any new trends, competitive information or market opportunities that you plan to exploit once you own the business.

This is a good time to connect the dots between the market opportunities you have identified and your plans for supplementing the product/service offerings to existing clients. The same applies to any new markets that you also plan to penetrate.

Build another table with three columns. The first column is the market opportunity and the second shows a summary of how the current owner deals with these market segments. For example, if they do not actively promote to that market, simply state that. The third column is where you summarize what you discovered about that market.

Marketing Strategy

Before: Tell the story of the current owner's approach to marketing and promotion. List the different advertising and marketing strategies used and what the results have been to date. Describe where the business currently resides including the appearance, access, location, and proximity to the market, parking availability, and exterior signs.

Show the current sales and distribution model that is used. State whether an outside sales team is responsible for market development. In the case of a retail business describe the role of location, advertising, and other marketing strategies.

Now describe the company's pricing strategy and how they are currently positioned. Identify the current strategy; i.e., do they target customers shopping for low price or do they use a value-added approach at a higher price?

Make a list of all the strategies and tools and how effective the current owner feels they have been. Include in your list brochures, Web site, advertising, radio, TV, newspaper, yellow pages, coupons, volume discounts, direct mail, and referrals. A good idea is to document the annual costs for each of the marketing tools and strategies employed by the current owner.

After: This will be a very valuable exercise because you now define specific promotional, advertising, and sales strategies you plan to use to expand your market and penetrate new ones.

This is an excellent place to state your plans for the location including any renovations you feel are required as as well as the exterior or interior signs. If you feel that there is a better location, describe your rationale for moving the business and include the difference in costs.

In a retail business describe any strategies you plan to employ including things like a loyal customer reward program. Make sure to include any software and computer technology upgrades that would be required.

As to the pricing of your products/services, reveal any opportunities you see to improve profit margins and how the business will be repositioned in the market and how this meets and serves the needs of the market. Look for an opportunity to reduce, consolidate, and reallocate marketing expenditures to be more in line with your overall marketing strategy. If there will be specific savings or additional expenditures, make sure to show the difference.

Do not forget to include an analysis of the current customer base/list. How will you use this list and what are your plans to take advantage of the change in management to consolidate your market position. If you have spoken with the top customers, do they plan to stay on with you after you assume control or state what you think will need to be done to maintain their business.

Management, Operations, and Organization

Before: Use a SWOT analysis (strengths, weaknesses, opportunities, and threats) to describe the current management situation. Where are the strengths and weakness? If there are threats to the viability of the business why do you think that management has chosen to not deal with the situation? If there are no job descriptions, comment about why that might be and the impact that has had on staff morale, productivity, and retention.

In terms of management structure, process, and systems explain how the business is managed. Define whether the business is highly controlled or whether there is a casual management style. If the business is managed by someone other than the owner, describe the management systems (if any) and also include staff views on this subject. Illustrate how the current owner makes use of professional services (if any, other than accounting) and the impact those services have had.

After: Point out the differences you will make in management style and systems. Show why the changes need to be made and your plans for making changes. Use the SWOT list from the Before section to show your plans.

If you plan to use a different approach to managing the business, then make sure to clearly define your approach and the major differences. Include staff, salespeople, customers, and financial management.

Your own resume is very important. Use the Resume Guide (Appendix H) to help you create your own resume to be included in this section.

Implementation Plan

This is your detailed project plan and tasks for the first 30 days. There is no need for a Before section as this deals exclusively with how you plan to manage the transition and implement your business plan.

I highly recommend that you create a calendar-based list of tasks. Make sure to include a list of tasks to maximize revenues in the first 30, 60, and 90 days of the takeover to avoid a drop in business volume.

This section should include a detailed list on the following major areas: sales, marketing and advertising, staff, staffing issues, systems, communication, bookkeeping, equipment, software, office, furniture, fixtures, land and buildings, as well as research and development.

This section will be a lot of work, but completing the analysis will make a very big difference in achieving a successful transition and maximizing your revenue opportunities. It is worth all the hard work and tedious process of making lists.

Potential Risks and Downfalls (Contingency Plan)

There is risk with every business venture. Deal with the issues in a factual and straightforward way. By being accurate in your assessment of the risks you can either plan ahead to eliminate them or have a plan to deal with them should they rise.

For example, make a list of things you can do if your competition starts to aggresively pursue your customers and staff. Show how you plan to reduce or eliminate identified risks or threats.

The Financial Plan

All your plans need to be reflected on the pro forma financial projections to make sure that your plans are properly resourced; otherwise they have no chance of success.

Print out your acquisition plan and reread it. As you do, mark down all the costs associated with the items in your plan. Then review your financial projections to make sure that you have not missed some important expenses.

Here you summarize acquisition and change costs, including all renovations, legal costs, as well as all your planned expenditures for a three-year period. Include the standard financial statements: i.e., balance sheet, income statement, cash flow, as well as a sensitivity analysis.

Appendix C
Due Diligence Checklist

Due Diligence is covered in detail in Chapter 20. As I explained, it is a good idea to create your own due diligence checklist that is specific to your industry and the business you are seeking to buy, but to help you get started, here are the major areas that you will want to check:

- Employees
- Management
- State employment laws
- Operations
  - Sales and marketing
  - Manufacturing
  - Inventory
  - Plant
  - Equipment
  - Customer service
  - Accounting and financial
  - Management
- Assets
- Liabilities
- Customer list

- Suppliers
- Financial review
- Inventory report
- Legal review
- Contracts and leases transferable
- Intellectual property

Appendix D
List of Legal Agreements

Numerous legal agreements are required in buying a business. The type of agreements used depends on your situation. You should see your attorney to find out exactly which ones he or she will prepare for you. Here are a few that may be mentioned:

Asset Sale Agreement

Entity Sale Agreement

Bill of Sale for Business Assets

Assignment of Lease

Assignment of Contracts

Assignment of Intellectual Property

Closing checklists

Confidentiality Letter

Covenant Not to Compete

Escrow Agreement for LLC Transfer Certificates

Escrow Agreement for Stock Certificates

Independent Contractor Agreement

Security Agreement for Asset Sale

Security Agreement for Entity Sale

Statement Regarding Absence of Creditors

Consent to Assignment of Contract

Consent to Sale of Assets by Corporate Board of Directors

Consent to Sale of Assets by Corporate Shareholders

Consent to Sale of Assets by LLC Members

Consent to Sale of Assets by Partners

Promissory Notes and Security Agreements

IRS 8594, Asset Acquisition Statement and Instruction

UCC Financing Statement and Addendum

Appendix **E**

Net Worth Statement Worksheet

Sample Net Worth Statement for
John and Mary Donald, December 31, 2004

Assets			Liabilities and Net Worth	
Cash		$9,000	**Mortgage Payable - Residence**	$189,000
			Mortgage Payable - Other	0
Liabilities				
Investments			Estimated Income Taxes	$26,000
Invested Assets - See Schedule	11,000		**Total Liabilities**	$215,000
Retirement Assets - See Schedule	132,000			
Goal Allocation - See Schedule	22,000			
Total Investments		165,000		
Real Estate				
Personal Residence		350,000		
Other Assets				
Automobiles	23,000			
Cash Surrender Value - Life Insurance	2,315		**Net Worth**	$331,000
Total Other Assets	22,000			
Total Assets		$546,000	**Total Liabilities and Net Worth**	$546,000

Appendix F

Transition Checklist

Once a deal has been arrived at and the seller has accepted your offer, it is time to create a checklist of tasks to be completed to ease the transition.

Attorney to Do

- Corporation: update minute book, resignation of director, appointment of new director or should we do a new corporation?

New Owner to Do

- Contact landlord for letter confirming that you can assume lease or sign a new lease.
- Prepare for staff meeting.
  - Meet with seller to create meeting agenda.
  - Discuss procedures to ease changeover.
- Staff announcement that a deal has been reached.
  - Introduce new owner.
  - Discuss time lines.
  - Discuss procedures to ease changeover.
- Finalizing the transaction.
  - New supplier accounts and numbers change.
  - Employer Tax ID number change (check with CPA).

- Seller pays all bills and obligations up to and including the date of takeover.

- Detailed inventory: products, equipment, office furniture, fixtures.

- Staff meetings.
  - Sales team: meet with sales team to discuss 30-day sales strategy.
  - Discuss and review announcement of new ownership and management.
  - Set appointments with each sales rep's major account to meet with owner.
  - Set sales quotas for each rep.

- New job descriptions or review of job descriptions.

- Employment contract?

Appendix G
Web Links

Greg Balanko-Dickson's Web site: www.gregbd.com

Business Planning Software: www.bplans.com

Business Search Engine: www.business.com

Online Business, Industry and Market Statistics: www.bizminer.com, www.valuationresources.com/

Online Legal Information: www.nolo.com

U.S. Small Business Administration: www.sba.gov

Canadian Government Business Gateway: www.businessgateway.ca; Business Information by Sector: strategis.gc.ca

Appendix H
Resume Guide

Format

Your resume should be no more than one page. Your full name, address, and contact numbers should appear across the top, followed by a short paragraph that contains a brief biography of your achievements and background that qualify you to own a business.

Highlights of Qualifications

This should be a bulleted list with more details that support the biography paragraph; the focus should be on the skills, experience, and education that would be an advantage to a future business owner.

Previous Businesses Owned

If you have been in business before, add a list of the businesses, achievements, and current status of the businesses. If the businesses have been sold, state when, and to whom.

Profile

This section is for unique qualities: for example, leadership, organization, communications, marketing, sales, planning, and financial analysis. Choose two of the top qualities or attributes that tie into your biography.

Employment Summary

Employment history should be brief with positions held and dates.

Education Summary

Formal education and degrees should be listed with year of graduation.

Index

About the Author

Greg Balanko-Dickson has worked as a consultant and seminar facilitator with hundreds of business owners in more than 30 different industries. He is a third-generation entrepreneur who has personally owned a number of different businesses and has been profiled in *Entrepreneur* magazine.